The Asymmetric Society

THE FRANK W. ABRAMS LECTURES

DATE DUE

The
Asymmetric Society

JAMES S. COLEMAN

SYRACUSE UNIVERSITY PRESS
1982

Copyright © 1982 by SYRACUSE UNIVERSITY PRESS
SYRACUSE, NEW YORK 13210

All Rights Reserved

First Edition

Library of Congress Cataloging in Publication Data

Coleman, James Samuel, 1926–
The asymmetric society.

(The Frank W. Abrams lectures)
Bibliography: p.
Includes index.
1. Social structure.   2. Interpersonal
relations.   3. Organizational behavior.   4. Social
role.   5. Social change.   I. Title.   II. Series.
HM131.C7419   305   81-23255
ISBN 0-8156-0172-7   AACR2
ISBN 0-8156-0174-3 (pbk.)

Manufactured in the United States of America

To my Mother, Maurine Lappin Coleman

JAMES S. COLEMAN received degrees from Purdue and Columbia universities and is Professor of Sociology, University of Chicago. He is the author of nearly 200 articles and chapters and 15 books, including *The Mathematics of Collective Action* and *Power and the Structure of Society*.

Contents

Foreword

*T*HE ABRAMS LECTURE SERIES is financed by a grant from the Exxon Education Foundation in memory of the late Frank W. Abrams, former chairman of the board of the Standard Oil Company (New Jersey), the predecessor of Exxon, and former chairman of the board of trustees of Syracuse University.

A member of Syracuse University's Class of 1912, Mr. Abrams was a life-long leader in support of higher education. He was a founder of the Council for Financial Aid to Education, chairman of the Ford Foundation's Fund for the Advancement of Education, and a trustee for the Alfred E. Sloan Foundation.

Mr. Abrams was one of the key pioneers who awakened American business, both through education and landmark legal precedents, to the need for financial support by business for private higher education. It was a contribution by Mr. Abrams, the importance of which cannot be overemphasized, which makes it particularly appropriate that this lecture series be presented in his name.

Special thanks are due the members of the Abrams Lecture Series Planning Committee, headed by Guthrie S. Birkhead, Dean of the Maxwell Graduate School of Citizenship and Public Affairs. Working with Dean Birkhead are Michael O. Sawyer, Vice-Chancellor of the University and Professor of Constitutional Law; L. Richard Oliker, Dean of the School of Management; Richard D. Schwartz, Ernest I. White Professor of Law; and Robert L. Payton, President, Exxon Education Foundation.

The Abrams Lecture Series has added a new and substantial component to the richness of academic life at Syracuse University. The 1981 series by James S. Coleman met the same high standards of the opening series in 1980 by Stanley Hoffmann. While their themes were totally different, each series dealt with a basic topic of enduring importance to the global community. Syracuse University and the Exxon Education Foundation are pleased to honor the memory of Frank W. Abrams in this way.

Melvin A. Eggers
Chancellor
Syracuse University

Preface

*T*HE AIM of the lectures on which this book is based, and the aim of the book itself, is to present a conception of the way society is coming to be organized, and to show some of the implications for the lives of ordinary people. The rapidity of social change has been sufficiently great to disorient us, to make us incapable of seeing how to direct that change toward a social system that will better serve us. The book is intended to present an orientation that will aid in directing that change.

Yet this orientation will not be a short course in introductory sociology, transmitting to you the consensus of sociologists about the way society is organized. From the very outset, I will describe to you a social structure that is not as most of my colleagues would see it, not something you could read about in popular expositions. I do this because I believe that fundamental to our ability to direct social change is a conception of the elements of which social structure is composed, and this is a task which has been rather neglected in sociological theory.

Indeed, an appropriate conception of the elements of which the social system is based is not only central to the practical task of directing social change; it is central to sociological theory, just as the comparable task is central to theory about any system of behavior. In physics, for example, arriving at an appropriate conception of the elements of which matter is composed has been for a number of years the preoccupation of the most highly theoretical segment of the discipline.

To engage in the task I have set is particularly pleasurable, for it allows simultaneous pursuit of fundamental questions in sociological theory, and of questions that have direct practical importance for the way we organize ourselves into societies or cope with the organization we find. The task is also part of a broader enterprise in the construction of sociological theory, in effect a second step in that enterprise. The first step was a series of four lectures given in the fall of 1971 at University of Pennsylvania, and published in revised form in 1973 as *Power and the Structure of Society*. These first two steps, nearly ten years apart, constitute in effect a prologue for a more extended work in sociological theory that is now in progress. I am grateful to the Exxon Foundation and to Syracuse University for providing the freedom of direction which allowed me to take this second step.

The chapters of the book constitute revisions, in some cases rather extensive, of the five lectures. The revisions were aided by comments from a stimulating Syracuse University audience in discussions which followed each lecture. Some of the comments raised in these discussions seem to me very useful to an understanding of the conception I have set forth in the chapters. Consequently, I have appended to each chapter a "Dialogue" based on the discussion following the lecture. Only those points in the discussion which serve to further extend and elaborate the ideas of the chapter — or in some cases, to present provocative challenges to those ideas — are included in the dialogues. I have added to the dialogues themselves at points, when additional dialogue would seem to further clarify or challenge the ideas of the chapter.

Fall 1981   James S. Coleman

The Asymmetric Society

1

Two Kinds of Persons
NATURAL AND CORPORATE

THE SOCIAL SYSTEM is constructed and inhabited by persons; yet it is different from the aggregate of psyches of those who inhabit it. A good illustration of this can be seen by the fall of once-great civilizations. For example, 400 years ago the Inca civilization fell to European conquest. What happened was that a rich social system, based on a delicate structure linking settlements at different altitudes and different latitudes, suddenly collapsed, leaving in its place a set of Indian villages living at barely subsistence level. What had changed was not the people but the social structure they inhabited. Yet the result of the change was an extreme difference in their way of life, in their resources and their opportunities.

So the proper task of the sociologist, a task that I will attempt to carry out here, is to describe that structure which we all inhabit, and which we call a social system.

What makes the task a confusing and difficult one, confusing even to some who call themselves sociologists, is that the social system is not only a structure constructed and inhabited by man; it is a structure of which persons themselves, each of us, you and I, are component parts. It is not like a house which we construct and inhabit but can then stand back from and observe as a structure composed of wood, brick, and other materials. Neither is it like other structures or systems which we did not ourselves construct, but like a house, can stand back from and observe: the structure of a chemical compound, the physiological system of a frog which we dissect, the subatomic structure of matter itself.

1

This *reflexive* character of a social system, if I may call it that, makes particularly critical what in some sciences is a very straightforward task: specifying the elements of which the system is constructed. One's first view of the matter might be the common-sense one: that persons are themselves the elements, the fundamental units of the system. That view has much to commend it for a single reason: persons are goal directed, acting to achieve some ends. Thus in a system composed of persons as elements, there is the possibility of goal-directed change, the possibility of man as the master of his fate. Theories of social change can, if the basic elements of the social system are seen to be goal-directed persons, contain a conception of directed change, not a conception of change arriving independent of man's will, with technology, or population density, or the physical environment as the engine of change. Conceptions of social change which do not have goal-directed persons as their fundamental units suffer the serious defect, from the point of view of each of us who does have goals, that man must be a passive bystander to the external forces of change.

The defect is even more fundamental. Such theories, in which goals or ends play no part, must themselves be silent in the evaluation of social states. They cannot distinguish, evaluatively, a social system established by Hitler in Nazi Germany, or a Jonestown, engaged in genocide, from any other. This is one reason why Marxist social theory remains attractive to many, even after a number of its specific propositions have proved to be invalid. It remains one of the few theories of social change which does have this evaluative character, grounded in what it describes as the "objective interests" of distinct social classes. Marxism presents a vision of the future —and no matter that the vision has proved to contain serious flaws, it remains for many better than a conception of social systems and social change in which man is a passive object of change brought about by external forces.

Yet the common-sense view that persons are the fundamental elements of which a social system is composed has a serious defect as well. To indicate what that defect is, I will describe some episodes of behavior and then ask a few questions about them.

Episode 1: A man living in a small community had died. His widow and son, neither of whom were well known in the community, were preparing for the funeral. The widow needed a pair of earrings for the funeral and went to the local variety store to buy a pair. The widow described to the saleslady, who knew of the man's death, that she wanted earrings for the funeral. They spoke for a moment about the man, who had been well liked in the community. The saleslady helped the widow in her attempt to select earrings, but the widow could find none that she liked. Then the saleslady said, "Why don't you borrow mine? They would be just right for the occasion." The widow assented, the saleslady took off her earrings, and the widow accepted them. The son watched all this.

Episode 2: Two men were sitting alone at separate tables in a dining room of the Hotel Europejski in Warsaw. Both were Americans, business visitors to Poland. One observed the other, as he ordered his meal from the waitress. It was apparent that the waitress knew some English, for she explained items on the menu. The waitress took the order, brought the food, and when the meal was finished, presented the bill, took the man's money, and brought him back the change. Then, as he prepared to leave a tip on the table before getting up to go, he asked the waitress about the location of the concert hall in Warsaw, where there was a symphony concert that evening. The waitress gave him directions and then offered some additional information: "They are playing an entire Mozart program this evening." The man hesitated, and as his compatriot observed from the nearby table, asked the waitress, "Would you like to come to the concert with me tonight?" Now the waitress hesitated, then went over to speak a few words to another waitress, returned, and replied to the man, "Yes, that would be all right." They arranged the details of how and when he would meet her. Then the man left his tip on the table, and as the other American watched from the nearby table, walked out of the dining room.

Episode 3: This episode is a personal experience. When I was in high school, I worked briefly in a neighborhood drug store behind the soda fountain. I had been instructed by another employee in tasks that I was to carry out: how to make an ice cream soda, a milk shake, an ice cream cone, and just how much ice cream there should be in each dip. I accomplished these things for the customers who came in, approximating reasonably well the service that I had seen my trainer carry out. Then a close friend of mine came into the drug store and asked for a vanilla ice cream cone with two dips. As I prepared to make the cone, I found myself confronted with a dilemma: should I give my friend extra ice cream in each of his dips, or should I give him just the amount I had been instructed to give, and had given to others? This was a very difficult dilemma indeed, one that bothered me greatly, as is evidenced by the fact that I still remember it.

Now what about these episodes? They were easily describable as interactions between two persons, with an added external observer in each of the first two episodes. They would hardly seem to constitute evidence (as, for example, something like the fall of the Inca civilization might) against a conception of persons as the elements of the social system, and relations between persons as the linkages which make a structure out of it. Yet each of them in its own way provides evidence in this direction. For in each, I will assert, there were not two persons in interaction but three. And there were in each of the first two episodes two interactions, not one. In the third episode there were three interactions.

The third "person" in the first episode was not the son; it was not a person at all, as you and I know persons, but was what the law at one time called a "fictional person," quite intangible, yet as much a party to the episode as both the widow and the woman who lent her the earrings. The third party was the variety store, and in the first part of the episode, the interaction was not at all between the widow and the other woman. It was between the widow and the variety store, with the saleslady only the *agent* of the variety store. Then suddenly when the saleslady showed the widow her earrings and suggested that she borrow them, a different interaction ensued. She was no longer acting as a saleslady, no longer an agent of the variety store, but a woman who, as a friend of the dead man, offered to lend her earrings to the widow. The interaction was now between the woman and the widow, two persons like you and me.

In the second episode a similar pair of interactions took place. First, the waitress was an agent of the Hotel Europejski as she took the order, explained the menu, served the food, and took the money for the bill. The money she took was not her money but was the property of the hotel. Her tip, which she picked up after the man had left, *was* her money, and she put it in a special pocket which contained money that was hers.

Again in this episode, there was a sudden shift from an interaction between the Hotel Europejski and the American customer to an interaction between a man and a woman. In this case it was initiated by the man, who had completed his interaction with the hotel and began one with the woman who was the waitress, by asking her to go with him to the concert. It may not have been so sudden as it appears, for there may have been, in the conversation about the location and content of the concert, minor intrusions of an interaction between the man and woman into the interaction between the man and the hotel. But whether it occurred in smaller steps or suddenly, there was a new interaction, and a new party to the interaction, the woman who was also a waitress.

It could, of course, have been more complicated than this, though an external observer had no way of knowing. That is, it could have been that the woman was also an agent of the state, and the man happened to be a person with information in which the state was interested. If that were the case, the second interaction of the episode was not as I have described it, between the man and the woman, but between the man and the state. If that were so, it would have been an especially interesting case, a case of mistaken identity: the man would have engaged in what appeared to him as an interaction with a woman, while the woman, as an agent of the state, would correctly see the interaction as one between the man and the state, with her only as agent. I raise this possibility for the additional theoretical insights it provides. As the possible complexity of the episode indicates, a person may be an agent for more than one corporate actor. In the classic case of the "double agent," though not in this example, the interests of these two corporate actors may conflict.

The third episode is somewhat different from the first two. When my friend came into the drug store, there were two interactions from the outset: one between my friend and the drug store, with me as agent, and the second between my friend and me. The dilemma I confronted was a moral dilemma. As agent, I had access to certain resources belonging to the drug store, in particular its ice cream. The moral dilemma was a question of whether I would use the drug store's resources to further my personal relation with my friend, or would not. Thus there was a potential third interaction as well, between the drug store and me, not as its agent but as a person who happened to have access to its resources: the possibility that I would steal from the drug store the extra ice cream that would benefit my relation to my friend.

What I have done in presenting these three episodes and explaining them as I have is to ask you to conceive of a social system as containing not only persons like you and me as its elements but also another kind of "person" as well: these intangible persons which the law once called "fictional persons" and I will call "corporate actors" to distinguish them from persons like you and me (whom the law calls "natural persons"). (I might not find it useful to do so if we all lived in communities like that of the dead man in Episode 1 and had little contact with those outside our own communities. For in such small communities, corporate actors are scarcely separable from the natural persons who go to make them up, and as in the episode, natural persons are never far below the exterior masks they wear as agents of corporate actors. But most of us do not live in such close communities, and even where those communities exist, their members have many relations that transcend community boundaries. In this larger social system that we all inhabit there are many actors, many parties to interactions, who are not of the natural person variety but are corporate actors.)

Corporate actors in many of their current forms are relatively recent components of social systems. It has always been the case, ever since a group of tribesmen banded together on a hunt to kill an elephant, that men have acted collectively toward a common goal. In that sense, we have always had corporate action, and by that token corporate actors. But until relatively recently in human history, these have been, with few exceptions, easily resolvable into the component persons of which they were composed, or easily identified with a particular natural person. That is no longer so, and it is coming to be less so all the time.

How did all this come about? A good way of tracing the emergence of the modern corporate actor, distinct and disembodied from any person, is through looking at the law. The law involves a particular set of actions, actions taken in the court as a response to actions that have been taken outside it: in civil actions persons sue and are sued; in criminal actions they are the objects of action by the state itself. If the law finds it unnecessary to conceive of persons other than natural persons, then this means that all actions can be traced back to natural persons: the law can find a defendent for an action and bring that person physically to trial. And before the thirteenth century western law found it unnecessary to conceive of persons other than natural persons. In the thirteenth century several new developments occurred which are reflected by changes in English law (and somewhat later on, on the Continent as well). The king had begun to issue charters to towns. Cambridge, for example, was chartered in the thirteenth century. What this meant was that a new actor came on the scene: a town could own tolls, could own land, could have a treasury. A town could sell or rent its tolls and rights of way, could enter into contracts. This meant that towns became parties before the court, as plaintiffs or as defendants. But if this were to be possible, the court had to find a new conception: an actor who could not be identified with any natural person but was somehow distinct, having its own rights and resources and its own interests (for the court had at times to determine whether the town's interests had been violated by the action of another party). All this seems reasonably simple from the perspective of the twentieth century; but it was not simple at the time, and there were many struggles to find a human person or persons behind the corporate body before the law gave in and recognized the town in itself as a "fictional person" or "legal person."

Charters to towns were one source of the new conception of a corporate actor distinct from any of the individuals who made it up. Another source on the Continent was the church. For a local church, originally established and provided with lands and other resources by a landed patron, slowly came to be detached from the patron, an autonomous entity. But as it did, and as it entered into contracts to buy or sell land, the puzzling question arose: who was it that was engaging in the contract? It was not the priest, for he was not a person before the law, owned no resources of his own, and was under the legal umbrella of the church. For a time the courts recognized legal fictions that we would smile at now: if a church was named St. Peter's Church, then "St. Peter" was the owner of the church property, the natural person to whom the church's action could be traced, no matter that St. Peter had been dead for more than a millennium. But as in the case of towns, the law began to recognize, from the thirteenth century onward, the church as a person before the law, which could act and be acted upon, and which had no physical body.

But the law did not just recognize those new forms of action that were going on in societies. It facilitated the new forms as well. As economic enterprise outgrew the family (which was the prototypical corporate actor of the Middle Ages, but one which was always traceable to a natural person, its head, and thus caused the law no problem), it became useful for several persons to join together to carry out the enterprise. They were able to do this only if they were protected from the liabilities that the joint enterprise might incur. In England, the law's recognition of a new class of persons facilitated this by making possible limited liability. Corporate debts and liabilities could reverberate backward toward the natural persons who had joined together, but they were stopped before they could reach all those persons' assets, for liability was limited to the extent of the original investment. This facilitated the growth of the great trading companies in England, such as the East India Company, and later facilitated the growth of the industrial revolution.

In other countries, where extended families were

stronger, corporate enterprise could take off from the oldest corporate form, the extended family, in the absence of a law of limited liability. In the thirteenth and fourteenth centuries the Medici bankers of Florence began in this way, as a direct outgrowth of the Medici family, and extended their activities to distant parts of Europe. In twentieth-century Japan, the modern Japanese corporation took its form — which differs considerably from that in the West — from the corporate character of the family, and corporate law became a natural extension of, or was grafted onto, family law.

In the United States, a corporate form in which the owners were especially far removed from the "corporation" was facilitated not only by limited liability, but by the fact that incorporation is done by states, rather than the federal government. States competed to have enterprises incorporate within them, by making laws of incorporation that were especially attractive to the corporations. And what was most attractive to those who ran the firms was to be as free as possible from the multiplicity of owners (or investors) which they had attracted. Delaware could probably be declared the overall winner in this competition, which took the form of allowing actions by majority rather than unanimity vote, allowing proxy votes, and allowing annual meetings of stockholders to be held in not easily accessible places and circumstances. The upshot of it all was that the corporation was much more readily freed to enter new forms of enterprise, to take chances, to fail more often than owners would like, but also to have more spectacular growth. It is no accident that Ralph Nader, searching for ways to make corporations more responsible, has recently proposed that powers of incorporation be removed from the states to the federal level.

But what does all this have to do with the widow in the variety store, or the waitress in the Hotel Europejski, or the boy making an ice cream cone in a drug store? The point of it all is this: the law has facilitated, and technological developments have motivated, an enormous growth of a new kind of person in society, a person not like you and me, but one which can and does act, and one whose actions have extensive consequences for natural persons like you and me.

Something of the character and nature of that growth can

FIGURE 1.1
Growth in Numbers of Corporations in the United States, 1916–1968

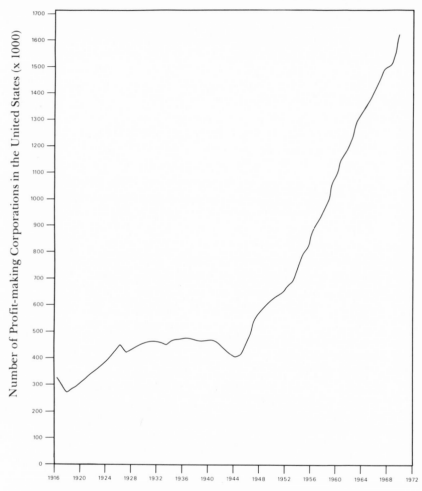

SOURCE: From Shi Chang Wu, "Distribution of Economic Resources in the United States," mimeographed (Chicago, Ill.: National Opinion Research Center, 1974).

FIGURE 1.2

Participation of Persons and Corporate Actors in Court Cases, New York State Court of Appeals, 1853–1973

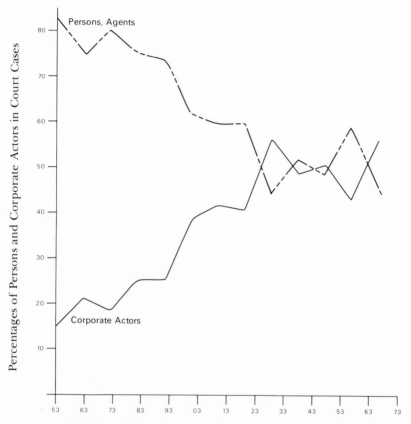

SOURCE: From Naava Binder Grossman, "A Study of the Relative Participation of Persons and Corporate Actors in Court Cases," mimeographed (Chicago, Ill.: National Opinion Research Center, 1974).

be seen by a few charts. Figure 1.1 gives an indication of the growth in numbers of profit-making corporations in the United States since 1917. The chart shows the numbers of corporations paying taxes in each year since 1917, a growth from 1917 to 1969 of more than five times. There was, to be sure, population growth among natural persons in the United

FIGURE 1.3

Attention to Persons and Corporate Actors on the Front Page of the *New York Times*, 1876–1972

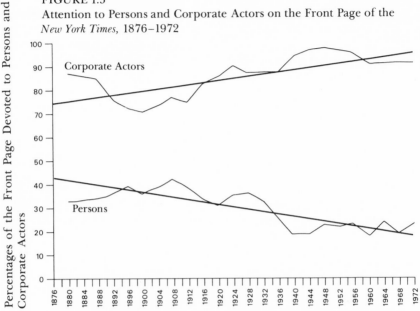

Percentages of the Front Page Devoted to Persons and Corporate Actors

SOURCE: From Ronald S. Burt, "Corporate Society: A Time Series Analysis of Network Structure," mimeographed (Chicago, Ill.: National Opinion Research Center, 1975).

States during this period, but far less than the fivefold growth shown in the chart.

Two other charts show something about the actions of corporate actors and persons. The first of these, Figure 1.2, covering all actions in the New York State Appellate Court from 1853 to 1973, shows the proportion of persons — or agents of corporate actors (the two were combined, because it was difficult to tell whether a person was a party to a case as a natural person or as an agent of a corporation) and the proportion that were corporate actors. The proportion was highly skewed in the direction of natural persons in 1853 (85 percent to 15 percent); by 1930, it became about even and has remained that way through 1973.

Figure 1.3 shows a different kind of action, that is, actions reported on the front page of the *New York Times*, over a portion of the same period, from 1876 to 1972. This chart shows the proportion of front page attention given—either as the subject of the action or as the object of action—to natural persons and the proportion of attention given to corporate actors—either the corporate actors or their agents. Again the chart shows a reduction in the proportion of all attention on the stage of the *New York Times* given to natural persons: from about 40 percent in 1876, down to about 20 percent in 1972.

What these changes suggest is a structural change in society over the past hundred years in which corporate actors play an increasing role and natural persons play a decreasing role. It is as if there has been extensive immigration over this period, not of persons from Europe or Asia or Africa or South America, but of men from Mars — a race of persons unknown in history. And this new race of persons has come to crowd out natural persons from various points in the social structure — at least some of those points that take part in activities which end up in appellate court or on the front page of the *New York Times*.

Yet these new persons are not Martians. They employ natural persons as agents, they have natural persons as their chief executives, they are governed by boards of directors made up of natural persons,* natural persons are their owners. Or so it once was; not even all these things are now true The stockholders are, with increasing frequency, themselves corporate actors, either other business corporations or other forms of corporate actors: pension funds or insurance companies. Members of their boards of directors may be agents of other corporate actors who are large stockholders.

---

*The practice in industrial firms of having executives of other firms or of financial institutions as members of boards of directors does not involve agency. These persons are board members in their capacities as persons, and their other positions are relevant only as they have acquired skills or knowledge from those positions. This points to a central difficulty of sociological studies of "interlocking directorates," which show the "interlock" created by an executive officer of one firm being a member of a board of directors of another firm. Because the board member does not come as an agent but as a natural person, there is no interlock in the sense ordinarily meant. It is for this reason that such studies have never proved very useful for the study of the functioning of society. The end point of such studies is ordinarily simply a demonstration of the "interlocks," with the implicit assumption that the interlock has significance for the functioning of society.

These corporate actors are different from those that have gone before in a fundamental way. In the earlier structure of societies, the family was the nucleus of the corporate structure, and the component elements of the family were natural persons. The family had a place in the larger structure, and through the family, each person did as well. That person had a fixed station and was an intrinsic part of the structure of society. As Marc Bloch (1961) wrote about the manor in the Middle Ages, "In the days when vassalage was developing, or when it was in its prime, the manor was first and foremost a community of dependents who were by turns protected, commanded, and oppressed by their lord to whom many of them were bound by a sort of hereditary link, unconnected with possession of the soil or place of abode" (p. 279). There were, to be sure, various devices to cope with the fact that persons were mortal, and one person's function might have to be taken over by another. But the central and overriding fact was that all social organization was organization of persons, and that those forms of organization which were fruitfully conceptualized as corporate actors were structures themselves composed of persons.

But the conception of the corporation as a legal person distinct from natural persons, able to act and be acted upon, and the reorganization of society around corporate bodies made possible a radically different kind of social structure than before. So long as society was seen as a single fixed organic whole, then the existence of social differentiation of activities as it was emerging in the Middle Ages (merchants, crafts, agriculture, churches) implied a rigid differentiation of persons in fixed positions — as in caste India, but with less continuity through generations. But as this differentiation of activities increased, a new form of social organization slowly came to be invented, and the law reflected this invention. This form involved the corporation as a functional element in social organization: a juristic person which could substitute functionally for a natural person. It could act in a unitary way, it could own resources, it could have rights and responsibilities, it could occupy the fixed functional position or estate which had been imposed on natural persons (and later it too could be partially freed from that fixed position). Natural persons, in turn, came to be free from the fixed estates, gaining mobility, as the structural stability of society was provided by the new fixed functional units, the corporations or corporate bodies. Persons needed no longer to be "one dimensional" but could occupy several positions in the structure at once and could change positions freely. It was the positions, as components of the new elements of society, the corporate actors, which provided the continuity and stability of structure.

The emergence of this new structure for society has had and continues to have extensive consequences for the lives of the natural persons within it, just as the fall of the Inca civilization had extensive consequences for the lives of the persons encompassed by that civilization. But these consequences come at differing rates, and many have yet to exhibit their full impact. Thus while we can point to the emergence of new structural forms in society beginning back in the eighteenth century (or even the thirteenth), many of the consequences are only now coming to be felt with any force; and others have yet to have their full impact. And there is not only the differing rate at which consequences come about; it is true as well that the change has not come all at once. We continue to have, in modern society, numerous corporate actors of the old form (the best example of which is the family), which are only over time supplanted by the modern corporate actor. And in different parts of society, the modern form of corporate actor has permeated to differing degrees. In the community in which the dead man's widow wore the saleslady's earrings, even apparently modern corporate actors (like the variety store, or like the city government) often function as if they were composed of persons rather than positions.

There are, as I have just suggested, corporate actors of an earlier form coexisting in society with the modern corporate actor. Although the family is the most important (and the one upon which I will focus in Chapter 4), the university is another. There are often events which clearly expose the structural difference between the university and a modern corporate actor; it is of some interest to examine one of these.

CIRCULAR A-21, AND A LIVING DINOSAUR

Recently, the Office of Management and Budget of the United States federal government issued a circular to universities receiving federal grants or contracts, labelled Circular A-21. This circular required that 100 percent of the time of all faculty members who had any portion of their salary paid by federal grant or contract funds must be accounted for, with accounts available to the government auditors. This circular touched off a strong negative reaction, not principally from university administrators but principally from faculty members. A portion of the reaction was due to the impropriety they perceived in the government's inquiry into what they regarded as a private matter between them and the university: their university activities covered by that fraction of salary not paid by the federal government. But part was due to a more fundamental matter, which requires for its understanding a return to the origin of universities in the Middle Ages. Universities were born before the modern purposive corporate actor, with its structure of positions devoted to a single central end, was conceived. A university was a collegium, a set of fellows who were *as persons* under the authority of the college, with the college's authority permeating all aspects of their personal lives. For example, as recently as the late nineteenth century, the fellows of colleges at Cambridge and Oxford could not marry. The exchange of time and effort for a salary was foreign to the very conception of the university, which had not even a central *purpose* as is true of modern corporate actors. The purposes of the university were contained within, and indistinguishable from, the purposes of the fellows and masters of which they were composed.

Universities have changed since the Middle Ages; but they have not become modern purposive corporate actors. They do not have a single central purpose; faculty members do not generally think of themselves as "employees"; rather, they are paid by the university to do that work which they themselves choose — in addition to teaching, which *is* a university purpose, but which many faculty members regard as a secondary portion of their university activity.* They have not made an exchange of time for money, they do not keep regular hours, they need not report to an administrator when they are to be away from campus for a period of time. There is no conception — by the university administration or by themselves—that they are paid for a certain number of hours of work.

Circular A-21 of the OMB, in contrast, implicitly assumes that the university is a modern purposive corporate actor like any other, with faculty members who are "employees," and who can reasonably be expected to account for 100 percent of the "university's" time. There is an impasse as fundamental as the difference between a family and a factory, for like the family, the university is built according to one set of principles, with roots predating the structure of modern society, and like the factory, OMB is built according to the structural principles of modern society.

It is not only Circular A-21 that creates problems for the structural principles of the university, for it has given up authority over the whole person and has not created a satisfactory substitute conception of the faculty members' obligations to the university. As a consequence, there are sometimes ad hoc and arbitrary regulations instituted. For example, Cambridge University has a rule that faculty members shall spend weekday nights in Cambridge during term, a regulation which has the practical consequence of preventing them from living in London and travelling to Cambridge only at the infrequent times that classes meet. Or Columbia University found it necessary to require one faculty member to report to the dean when he was to be absent from campus for more than a week. Or another university found that it had a faculty member who was simultaneously being paid as a "full-time" faculty member at a second university. And many universities

*An interesting illustration that the distinction between faculty member and employee has not completely vanished can be found on signs in the parking lots at Johns Hopkins University (which retains more of the classical structure than do most American universities). Some are marked "Employees"; others are marked "Faculty Members."

have fixed limits to the number of days that their faculty members may be paid for outside consulting, such as a "one day a week" rule. This odd rule is, of course, to escape requiring that the faculty member spend four days on campus, or four days at university work—to maintain the understanding that the faculty member does not owe the university a prescribed amount of time or effort. Yet it of course can be even more confining, because it carries the implication that the university also has rights to proscribe work for pay on the sixth and seventh days of the week or at night.

It may well be that there are more benefits than costs to the university's structural fault, though the university may experience the costs and others the benefits. Many of the technological innovations since World War II, ranging from computer technology to gene-splicing, have occurred in universities. And their exploitation has often been through an enterprise begun by faculty members — who were not prevented, by an employment relation or by ad hoc rules devised by university administrators or OMB, from engaging in such enterprise. The usual employment relation, by contrast, explicitly forbids any entreprenurial activity related to the content of the employee's work.*

It is clear from the examples of university administrators' efforts to limit outside activity that Circular A-21 of OMB, however foreign to the university's conception of itself as a community of scholars, and to the faculty member's conception of his work as self-directed and self-determined, has merely exposed a structural fault in the university resulting from the incongruity of the social structure in which it grew up and the social structure in which it now finds itself. How the university will change, and how the modern corporate actors surrounding it will themselves change, is not clear; but the university's presence in modern society serves as a re-

*It could well be that a change in this relation, to allow joint ventures by the corporate actor and the employee which would exploit the employee's innovations, is the next major change in structure of the business corporation. Donald Schon (1971) used the example of the 3M Company as an indicator of this possible future pattern.

minder that modern purposive corporate actors are not the only form of social organization. When I examine, through this book, consequences of these structural changes for the lives of natural persons who inhabit the structure, I am not discussing consequences with which we have lived for a long time. I will rather be discussing changes that are current, as well as some changes we have only begun to experience. Yet it is the fact that man is goal directed and has the capacity to direct the changes that occur in society that makes these changes that I will describe not inexorable, but subject to man's will. It is only this fact which makes such an enterprise worthwhile. For if we could do nothing other than watch the waves of change wash over us, then a better view of the oncoming waves would hardly be of value.

In the succeeding chapters I will focus in some detail on a few of the consequences of this pervasive structural change in society. In what remains of this one, I want to point briefly to two of those consequences, one having to do with asymmetry in relations, and the other the nature of authority. In this way, I hope to give a sense of the importance of the changes that follow upon the structural change I have described. And I hope to raise in your mind the question of whether we have reached a social structural equilibrium — and if not, what the future might hold.

THE ASYMMETRY OF RELATIONS

The first and perhaps most compelling attribute of the modern social structure which we inhabit is the *asymmetry* of a large portion of its relations. I can best describe this asymmetry to you by asking you to look at the diagram of Figure 1.4. What I have done here is to start with the recognition that there are two fundamentally distinct types of actors in modern society, natural persons and corporate actors. Then I have classified actions according to whether the *subject* of action is a person or corporate actor, and according to whether the *object*

FIGURE 1.4

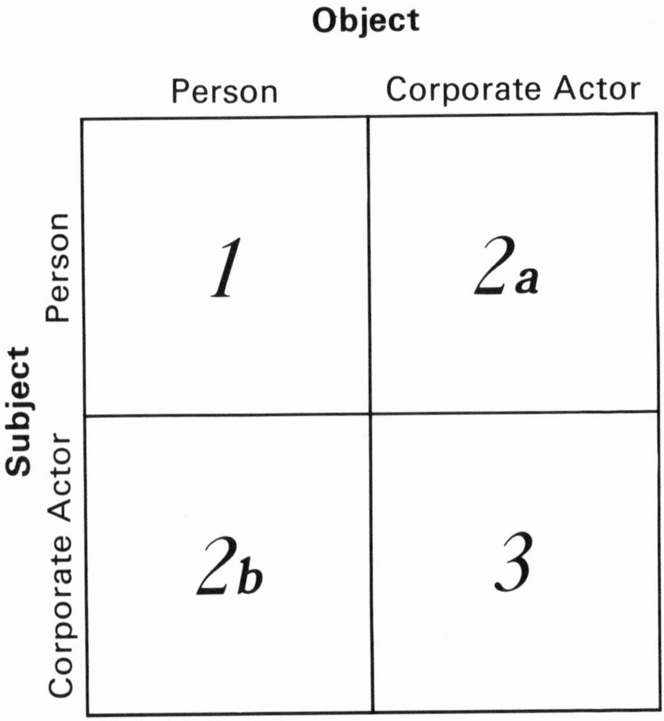

Object

	Person	Corporate Actor
Person	*1*	*2a*
Corporate Actor	*2b*	*3*

of action is a person or corporate actor. The result is four kinds of action, which I have labelled 1, 2a, 2b, and 3. Actions of type 1 are actions to which we have all been socialized as children: actions of one person toward another person. Actions of type 3 are actions of a corporate actor toward another corporate actor, for example an action of one corporation toward another, or an action of the state (that is, the government) toward a corporation or a trade union. Actions of types 2a and 2b, however, are actions in which the two parties to an action are of *different* types: one is a person and one is a corporate actor. And because a relation involves both parties as subject and object of action, we may speak of a relation of type 2, involving actions of types 2a and 2b. This, in contrast to the other two types of relations, is asymmetric. And with the enormous growth in numbers of corporate actors in modern society, this asymmetric form of relation has come to proliferate throughout the social structure. Some of the growth in appearances of corporate actors in court cases which I presented earlier is growth in this kind of relation, a person and a corporate actor opposed in court. Some of the growth in attention to corporate actors in the *New York Times*, which I also presented earlier, is growth in this kind of relation, that is, articles involving some sort of interaction or relation between a person and a corporate actor. Yet either of these is only a pale reflection of the total growth that has taken place in these asymmetric relations.

Increasingly, there are relations like those exemplified in the three episodes I described, relations which at first glance appear to be between two persons, but in fact are between a person and a corporate actor, with the corporate actor represented by its agent. Yet the three episodes are not typical of the type-2 relations, for many of these relations are not only asymmetric in the types of parties they involve, but are asymmetric—often extremely so—in two other respects as well: in the relative *sizes* of the two parties, and in the *numbers* of alternative transaction partners on each side of the relation. Typically, the corporate actor is very large in resources, compared to the person on the other side of the relation. On one side may be the telephone company, a corporate actor, and on the other side, a customer, a person. Or on the one side may be the United Steelworkers' Union, a corporate actor, and on the other side a union member, a person. Or on the one side may be the United States government, a corporate actor, and on the other side, a citizen, a person.

And typically, on the corporate actor side there are only a few other parties as alternative transaction partners (or as in the illustrations I have just given, there may be none). On the person side there are typically hundreds, thousands, or even millions. These two asymmetries have extensive consequences for the nature of the relation. One consequence is that the corporate actor nearly always controls most of the conditions surrounding the relation. The corporate actor controls much of the information relevant to the interaction — typically by advertising, propaganda, market research, public opinion research, credit ratings of customers, and dossiers of other sorts. Information expressly designed to serve the interests of the person is far less in evidence. And as with information, so with other of the conditions. The end result is that two parties beginning with nominally equal rights in a relation, but coming to it with vastly different resources, end with very different actual rights in the relation.

These asymmetries of power in relationships have led to extensive attempts by persons to redress the balance, using as their instrument the state. Thus the principle of *caveat emptor*, let the buyer beware, in a social structure which was not asymmetric between buyers and sellers, has been replaced, in the asymmetric society, with sharp restriction of the seller's rights and expansion of the means of redress for persons. The last decade alone saw a whole spate of such legislation at both the state and federal levels, ranging from truth in lending laws to privacy acts, designed to protect natural persons from corporate actors' use of information about them in ways antagonistic to their interests.

The asymmetry, however, has other consequences in the behavior of the two parties to the relation. The person, if unconstrained by internal moral constraints, may steal from or cheat a corporate actor, protected by the anonymity provided by numbers. A person angry at the telephone company might rip the cord from a public phone, or a customer or employee in a store may shoplift, or may fail to notify a cashier if too much change has been returned. Yet these same persons might never do any of these things in relations with other *persons*, where actions are subject to the other's constant surveillance.

In short, the asymmetry of the relation gives power to the corporate actor and at the same time gives opportunities for malfeasance to the person. On both counts, the relation functions less well than the personal relations of which social structures have long been composed, and for which normative systems of constraints have arisen.

The asymmetries of size, and their consequences, can be found also in type-3 relations, in which both parties to the relation are corporate actors. Just as natural persons and corporate actors characteristically differ in their sizes, different corporate actors engaged in a relation are often of different sizes. This can have important consequences, for a relation between two corporate actors is often a link in a long chain of production.

ASYMMETRY AND POWER IN LONG CHAINS OF PRODUCTION

In the economy the full freedom of corporate actors to engage in various kinds of activities, together with economies of scale in specialized activities, has meant a continuing tendency for productive activity to be divided into ever more specialized links in a productive chain. Insofar as these are carried out by distinct corporate actors, not merged through vertical integration, then there will be, in the production of a given good, different sized actors at each point in the chain. Now if we conceive that at each point there is value created by the activity — corresponding closely to the concept of value added at each stage of production — then we can see the corporate actor within which that value has been created as a "partitioner" of the value among the different transaction partners, for example, labor, stockholders, customers, suppliers. If the power of an actor in a transaction is largely a function of its size, then we can expect that the fraction of that value added which will go to a given partner will be large if it is larger (i.e., more powerful) than the corporate actor, smaller if it is smaller than the corporate actor. If the corporate actor is more powerful than any of its partners, then it will be a "value sink," absorbing surplus value for its own growth. If it is owned by a single strong owner, it will give up more value to the owner; if its labor is highly organized, it will give up more value to its labor in wages; if, as is sometimes true, the customer is larger and more powerful, or the market is highly competitive, it will give up value to the customer, in the form of lower prices; if its suppliers are larger than it is, it will give up more value to its suppliers, acceding to the terms of the transaction they set.

The end result will be a drift of this newly created value to certain points in the production chain. Value will drift toward those nodes that are the most powerful, which ordinarily means the largest nodes. If these nodes are at the starting points of the production line, as in lumber products, for example, then greater value is asorbed there. If they are at an intermediate stage, as the automobile companies and United Auto Workers are in the chain of automobile production, or the food processor (or in some cases food retailer) is in the chain of food production, then greater value will be absorbed at that intermediate stage. If the largest actor or the most competitive market is the final consumer, then greater value will be absorbed there.

This drift of value means also inequality. It means, for example, that employees of automobile firms, from managers to workers, are paid more than they could get for comparable work in another industry, and the corporation itself becomes even wealthier. It means that inequality is created in society, inequality not due to differences in skill or in effort but to one's particular location. Just as some persons in the old social structure have had the good fortune to be born into wealthy or powerful families, some persons in the new social structure have the good fortune to be at a node which, larger than those which surround it, can extract a greater fraction of the value from the transactions it engages in than can those with which it deals. And it means that inequality among corporate actors has a natural tendency to increase. For the larger the corporate actor, the more likely that it will be larger than its transaction partners, and thus able to increase its size still more.

Not only do the type-2 and type-3 relations show a size asymmetry between the two members of the relation. The relation also takes different forms. Corporate actors differ, with business corporations, associations such as trade unions, and the state itself as three examples. And the kinds of relations of persons to corporate actors differ as well. Persons are employees, they are customers, clients, citizens, members, managers, officials, stockholders. Three general classes of relations of persons to corporate actors are important: those that occur in a *market* structure (as, for example, a corporation-customer relation), those that occur in an *hierarchical* setting (as, for example, a relation between a bureaucracy and an office holder), and those that are what might be described as *communal*. This last requires explanation in some detail, and in fact, the general discussion of market, hierarchical, and communal relations between corporate actors and persons must be an extended one if we are to see some of the consequences of asymmetric relations for persons in modern society. This is best done, however, in the discussion of rights and responsibilities in an asymmetric society, and I will reserve that discussion for the next chapter. For the present, I want to turn to a central feature of any social structure — authority—and to ask how that has changed with the change from the old social structure—in which persons like you and me were the sole elements of the structure—to the new, in which a different sort of person—the corporate actor I have been examining—constitutes a central element.

THE FREEDOM FROM ABSOLUTE AUTHORITY

In the old social structure, before invention of the modern corporate actor, the *person* was an element in the structure of social action. Now, the person is merely an occupant, and the position which that person fills is the element of the structure of social action. A consequence of central importance is that the person, *as* a person, is now free. When it was the person who was the element of the structure, then the exercise of authority over action meant the exercise of authority over the person. This had its compensations: the party in authority over the person ordinarily had some responsibilities for the person as well. But the person was still not free. And this subjection to absolute authority had just those consequences that are most often associated with slavery: the unfree person subject to the arbitrary will of the master, sometimes impeded by humanitarian concerns but sometimes not.

With the invention of the modern corporate actor and its pervasive spread across all areas of action, freedom was no longer limited to those artisans or traders who were self-employed and those of high estate. Freedom became universal, for a person was no longer part of an organic hierarchical structure but was in a free and open market, free from the master and able to sell his services and exercise choice in doing so. A person's effective choice has been great or small depending on the kind of labor he could supply and the demand for that kind of labor, a demand which if small can obscure the fact of freedom itself. But the freedom is there, and there seems little possibility of a return to a social structure in which persons are subject, as whole persons, to the pervasive authority of other persons. For no one except children does such a structure remain in modern society, and even that becomes increasingly problematic, except at the youngest ages.

THE IRRELEVANCE OF PERSONS

But there is another edge to the sword: the person is not only free; he is irrelevant in a fundamental sense. The person is merely an occupant of a position in the structure and can at any time be replaced. Persons have become, in a sense that was never before true, incidental to a large fraction of the productive activity in society. This is most evident when the person who occupies a position in a corporate actor is replaced not by another person but by a machine. Then the general irrelevance of persons is clear. But the invention which made this possible was not a technological invention which replaced man by machine; it was a social invention which created a structure that was independent of particular persons and consisted only of positions. Once this was done, it became merely a matter of ingenuity to devise machines that could carry out the activities which those positions required.

The irrelevance of persons in the structure is not a question of machines, it is a question of the *form* of the structure. In management training programs in many firms, there is a game that is used as part of the training program: the in-basket game. In this game the management trainee is asked to assume that he has unexpectedly replaced the previous plant manager over the weekend and is confronted with the unanswered mail in his predecessor's in-basket. The task is to respond appropriately to the various items of correspondence. A few are personal, and he is expected to distinguish between those and the correspondence that is intended for the plant manager as manager, that is, as agent of the firm. The aim of the in-basket exercise is to make the transition from one manager to the next unnoticeable — to make the manager *as a person* irrelevant to the functioning of the plant. This is good for the smooth functioning of the organization; but it takes away something of central importance to each of us: the sense of being *needed*. It is this which makes the family—which is an anachronism from another age in the modern social structure we have created—an important element in our lives. A family member is a part of that family as a person, not as an occupant of a position; and no answers to correspondence in an in-basket can make a family's loss of a member unnoticeable.

AUTHORITY OVER ACTIVITIES

But there is another point about authority. The freedom from absolute authority that modern corporate actors have brought, and the general irrelevance of persons to the structure of social action, does not mean that authority relations have vanished. The facts are very different indeed.

Let me return to the three episodes with which I began. As I indicated earlier, in each there were at least two relations: one between two natural persons, and one between a natural person and a corporate actor. But the corporate actor is intangible and must act through its agent: the variety store had its saleslady, the Hotel Europejski had its waitress, the drugstore had its counterboy. The result was that each of three natural persons was acting in the interest of another — not out of altruism, of course, but for pay. Each had made a transaction with the corporate actor, involving an exchange of time and effort for money — a transaction that each person in society who is an *employee* makes, for as an employee, one's time and effort are being employed to another's ends.

Because each of these three persons, as an employee, is acting in the interests of another, there is a continual conflict of interest within the person, between his *own* ends and those of the corporate actor whose agent he is. In each of the episodes, that conflict of interest was apparent: the saleslady might have made a sale for the store had she not offered to lend her earrings; the waitress neglected the restaurant's other customers (among them the other American sitting nearby and observing) while she carried on her personal transaction with the American customer; and the counterboy at the drug store was confronted with a moral dilemma created by the conflict of interest.

This conflict of interest that resides in each person who is an employee has one structural consequence: each must be supervised. If the conflict is to be resolved in the direction of the corporate actor, and the time and effort not stolen back by the employee, nor other resources stolen by the employee, supervision and authority must be exercised over that employee's activities. The saleslady has her supervisor, the waitress has her head waitress, the counterboy has the manager or the pharmacist to supervise his activities.

What is insufficiently recognized is that this was not always the case. In earlier social structures, a person was either free or unfree. If free, he worked for himself, for his own ends. He was taxed, of course, on the fruits of his labor, as we are today. But like today's farmer or dentist or doctor or novelist, who work for themselves, and unlike today's clerk or engineer or machinist or manager or secretary, his daily activities were spent in pursuit of his own ends, not those of another. If he was not free, and in thirteenth-century England, something more than half were not, his whole person was under the authority of another. Thus we can say that in the old social structure, a part of the population, in fact the larger part, was much less free from the authority of another than is the average person today; but at the same time, a portion of the population was *more* free from the authority of another than is the average person today. Again Karl Marx, who stood at the juncture between the old social structure and the new, recognized that the contractarian political philosophy of liberalism, or as Harold Laski (1917) and C. B. McPherson (1962) called it, the philosophy of "possessive individualism," allowed a man to sell his freedom in return for a money wage. Marx saw this as a return to servitude, and of course to some degree it is. It is a very peculiar form of servitude: a *person* is not under authority of another, as was the case in the old social structure; rather, a portion of the persons's activities—that portion which he has exchanged for a wage—is under authority of another.

Even more can the contrast be made with the recent past, for in America, from the beginning there has been a steady decline in the proportion of persons working for their *own* ends, under their own authority, and a steady increase in the proportion of persons who work for the ends of another, under the authority and supervision of another. The fraction of the population that consists of farmers, proprietors, craftsmen, and other self-employed persons, has declined since America became a nation.

The end result is that a very large part of the action that is carried out in society, and by far most of the economically productive action, is action carried out by one person to accomplish the ends of another — the corporate actor whose agent he is. And it means that a very large fraction of persons in society are spending a large portion of their time not acting toward ends which they themselves have but toward the ends of another. Even more, they are spending this time under the authority of another, their activities supervised by an agent of the corporate actor who of course must himself be supervised.

Is this a desirable state of affairs for society? I think not. Yet it is a state of affairs which follows directly from the structure of corporate action which we have invented for ourselves and under which we live.

Is it the end state? Is the social invention of the modern corporate actor — which has given us natural persons a freedom our forefathers never had, but has placed many of us in impersonal, often inhuman bureaucracies — the last such social invention? Or is there a possibility of a more attractive future, following still another social invention? I think there is; I think some of the outlines of such a social invention are beginning to emerge, and I will say something more about such a vision of the future. But before it is possible to do that, it is necessary to say something more about the present: how corporate actors have acquired their rights, and how they use those rights; what kinds of relations corporate actors other than the state have to the state; and what is their impact on certain activities that are central to the continuation of society — in particular, the regeneration of society through new generations of natural persons.

After examining these matters I will return in succeeding chapters to the questions I have just raised. Only then will I be in a position to express optimism or pessimism about the social structure we will inhabit in the future.

DIALOGUE 1

Q: I would like to suggest — let me take a minute or so to justify my claim — that what you have done is to take a middle range, holist position, not at a level that Hegel would have, perhaps. You have said that there are things that you call "corporate actors." They sound like organizations of one kind or another to me, and that would do, I think, as well; but I think you've been a little bit over-influenced by the legal status, the legal definition of these "people," the corporate actors — now I'm doing it, too — and I think you have not taken account of the fact that any organization, any corporate actor, which is void of ordinary persons, would cease to have any effect. While it's true that some significant number of normal persons can be replaced in an organization, I cannot understand how an organization can be void of persons. What you're doing, then, is not showing a sufficient willingness to get inside that legal person, to look at the way in which its face to the rest of the world can be built up with individuals as basic components which come together and behave in a certain way subject to certain agreements among them.

A: What you say is both correct and incorrect. Such examination of the internal structure of corporate actors certainly is a major task for any social theory which attempts to account for what goes on in society. That is, it is necessary to look at the way in which corporate actors come to take action. Sometimes this is not as simple as it seems. It is not merely the direction of the man at the head.

There are other forces. For example, John R. Commons (1924), describing the way in which trade unions function, reported what a trade union leader had told him about how decisions were made in the union. He said they had a special term. They first of all talked to "the action." They used the term "action" as a noun. What they meant was, "Consult with persons to the degree that those persons in the union were important to the functioning of the union." Adolph Berle and Gardiner Means (1940) used a similar term in discussing the way in which modern corporations come to take action. So in that sense you are correct.

At the same time, it is important to distinguish actions of persons as persons, although they may be in an organization, from their actions as agents of the organization. That is a fundamental distinction, and one which, in some social theory, is not observed. For example, even Peter Blau (1964), who is one of the best social theorists, in his book *Exchange and Power in Social Life,* discusses primarily the *personal* relations of persons within an organization and the power relations among those persons. He neglects the way in which persons' actions combine in one way or another, as agents in the employ of an organization, to lead the corporate actor to take action. Without a conception of the corporate actor *as* actor, having the same status in social theory as natural persons in their capacities as actors, the theory is crippled, and blind to a large part of the action that takes place in modern society.

Q: But if, for you, there are natural persons and corporate actors, what about the class action suit? The notion of a "class" in the idea of a class action suit is neither a natural person nor a simple aggregate of natural persons, nor is it a corporate actor. It is perhaps a definition of a common interest, but the emergence of class action suits suggests that the somewhat abstract notion of a common interest will increasingly become solidified as a legal device somewhere between the natural person and the corporate actor.

A: Now, in order to answer you, I must refer to a special corporate actor, the state. In the past decade and a half there have been a large number of actions taken by the state, in response to demand by natural persons, to restrict the rights of corporate actors other than itself. The legal permissibility of class action suits is one of those. Class, as you say, is a very interesting concept. As it is used in class action suits, it is more like Arthur Bentley's (1908) old concept of interest than anything else. It is not truly an actor, in the sense that except in the court case, it does not take unitary action, but is an object of action. That is, all members are argued to have been affected by an actor's action. This is similar to one of the ways that modern corporate actors came into existence — for example, being acted upon as a single entity by the king. Yet there is a difference. To have experienced similar consequences from a single actor's actions (as did the families of Thalidomide babies, for example) is not the same as being acted upon as a single entity. The members of a class have similar interests but not a single joint interest, except in one outcome, the court's finding the defendant liable.

Q: Even though your ideas might be generally acceptable to someone who takes a legal standpoint, such a person would treat the state as quite distinct from the other actors, and except in what you have just said, it seems to be quite clear that you are not distinguishing the state.

A: Of course, I distinguish the state only when it suits my ends to do so. The state is, as you say, a very different kind of corporate actor from the others. All others are in some fashion subordinate to its will. That makes for some interesting questions about the character of corporate actors in different kinds of states, and I will have more to say about that.

Q: Now to turn to your empirical information. It does not seem to me that you have shown that there are increasing proportions of corporate actors in society, only that the New York Times, *legal personnel, corporate personnel, and so forth, increasingly treat corporate actors. Do corporate actors have any objective reality in your view, aside from these conventions of language? There is another way to ask this question that might make it clearer: do you mean "corporate actor" in the usual sense of the term "actor," that is, decision maker?*

A: Yes, I do mean exactly that. In fact, the reason I do not use the term "organization," which refers to much the same entities as does "corporate actor," is because "organization" does not carry the connotation of unitary action. What makes an entity a corporate actor—and there are a variety of different kinds — is *action*. One can also use other kinds of indicators—whether there are resources that are seen as belonging to the corporate actor, for instance. But the essential point is that if there is coherent, goal-directed action, there must be an actor. The actor has a social reality, whether or not we can point to a physical body.

Q: You seem to be ambivalent about whether natural persons or corporate actors are in control. You argue that persons are free but irrelevant in the new social structure; but then you suggest that an exercise of human will may lead to social inventions that lead to a more attractive future. Which is it?

A: That is up to us natural persons. Unless we begin to direct ourselves to the question of what kinds of social structures we are inventing and thereby coming to inhabit, we may permit social structures that are very difficult to change — because once an actor is in existence it has strong interests in survival, and will direct its resources toward that survival. It is exactly the raising of these questions to which my efforts are directed. To correctly perceive the changes that are taking place will, I think, give us the possibility of directing our future, in a structural sense, more than we might otherwise be able to do. It is not inevitable that we will go in the direction each of us would prefer to go, because in fact we may not be able to act as a unitary actor toward a goal.

Q: Now to turn to a different question. Suppose I accept your conception of the "corporate actor." You seem to see the modern corporate actor, as you have described it, as an inevitable result of something called "development." Are there not alternative ways in which a nation or society can be said to be developed or modern without the emergence of the corporate actor?

A: I do not see it, in all its details, as inevitable. Some of the modified forms of development that are taking place in various parts of the world suggest variations upon the modern corporate actor as it exists in the developed countries of the West. The structural constraint imposed by economic development is probably less than we have believed in the past. I do not have a prescription for what is possible; we are, of course, learning about some possibilities from modified forms of corporate action that are coming into existence around the world. I did not, in any examination of corporate actors, discuss law, other than English law or Continental law. Islamic law, for example, does not have a concept of a corporate actor other than the extended family. This is merely one illustration of the fact that the conception of corporate actor has developed to different degrees and in different ways in different legal systems. Whether Islamic law is compatible with modern economic development without undergoing extensive modification is, however, doubtful.

Q: For the present to suppose that I accept your conception of "corporate actors." It may not be harmful to the long-run interests of natural persons for there to be a structure with both natural persons and corporate actors. In a government bureaucracy there are bureaucrats or administrative elites that are indifferent to the political structure and power and pressures of the time, and that have as their sole concern the operations of the corporation, the government. Might it not be to our advantage to have people in corporate structures be unaffected by the power of natural persons?

A: Let me understand you. You are suggesting that bureaucrats are a kind of prototypical agent, and that natural persons may be altogether better off by having such agents

unresponsive to personal "connections." Under some conditions, yes. But there is first the fact that most bureaucrats do
not act as pure agents. What we think of as the undesirable
characteristics of bureaucrats are in fact the ways in which the
interests of the person who is in the position come to distort
and impede the functioning of that person as an agent of the
corporate actor (see, for example, Merton, 1952). It is the
inappropriate incentive structure, or reward structure, within
the corporate actor which makes the person who occupies a
position in the corporate actor act in a self-protective way.
These actions are not those of the pure agent; they may be
damaging to the interests of the corporate actor, or to the
interests of the client which the corporate actor is attempting
to serve, or to both.

   *Q: You have suggested that there is a hierarchy of the natural
person, the corporate actor, and the very special corporate actor called
the state, which is hierarchically above other forms of corporate actors,
such as business and labor. Yet today we see more and more the growth
of multinational corporations, which themselves have powers and authority beyond the legal constraints of the state. Perhaps the state is not
more powerful. We may be seeing what could be called the obsolescence
of the nation-state.*

   A: You have made an interesting point. There is an
emerging conflict between two entities, both of which are relatively recent upon the historical scene, the nation-state on
the one hand, and multinational corporations on the other
hand. The state, of course, because it has coercive powers and
controls the means of legitimate violence, does have a special
position. But the question of how the conflict between the
nation and the multinational corporation is going to be resolved in the long run seems to me open.

   *Q: I want to raise here a fundmental doubt. Perhaps the distinc-
tion you make between natural persons and corporate actors is artifi-
cial. In the examples you have mentioned, while the actions of people
as agents are quite clear, it's not clear that when they step out of that
particular role, they are acting simply on their own behalf. The
woman in the jewelry store is acting as a friend of the family, for
example. People act in various social contexts, as a student or profes-*

sor, as a member of various kinds of organizations, as a member of a class. Persons act in a variety of roles. Therefore, perhaps one might say either that there is no such thing as a natural person per se *or, to look at the obverse, corporate actors* per se *really are nothing more than very complex congeries of individuals.*

A. It is true that one could conceive of matters that way. What you describe is in fact very much the way role theory in sociology has proceeded. That, however, is one of the many blind alleys that social theory has taken. The essential question is this one: what will be a fruitful way to describe the structure of the social system? I believe that it is fruitful to describe the structure of a system in terms of action. To describe it in terms of action one has to identify actors, and then one arrives, by successive steps, at the position that I have taken. My disagreement with what is characteristically called role theory is that many activities which are described as roles, such as the role of the woman as friend of the family, are not roles in the same sense as her role as saleslady. In her role as saleslady she is an occupant of a position in an actor. In the other, it is her whole person, including her personal interests, which is involved in the interaction. This may turn out not to be a productive way to look at things, but I believe that it will be.

2

Sovereignty and Rights

IN CHAPTER 1 I described a paradox of modern society: the new social structure, with its corporate actors which are independent of particular persons, has freed man from a sometimes oppressive structure of the sort that existed in the Middle Ages. Yet the resulting situation is one in which most natural persons are *employed* by these impersonal corporate actors, and thus find themselves working for ends that are not their own. And both in the employment relation and in many of our other relations, as customers, clients, citizens, we natural persons find ourselves in a relation with an impersonal entity that is much larger and more powerful than we.

The question then becomes whether we can devise a social structure that does not contain this paradox. We live in what I called the "new" social structure. But are there further social inventions which will give a social structure that is more satisfactory to natural persons than the one we now inhabit?

The search for an answer to that question involves an examination of rights. Corporate actors, as entities created by persons, take a particular form under a particular allocation of rights. To learn more about the form necessitates learning more about the structure of rights under which a given form arises. And a useful place to begin is back in the thirteenth century, before the old social structure had begun to give way to the new. The old social structure is reflected in this quotation from the F. Pollock and Frederic Maitland (1898), writing of the thirteenth century and describing the "sorts and conditions of men."

37

Of the divers sorts and conditions of men our law of the thirteenth century has much to say; there are many classes of persons which must be regarded as legally constituted classes.
Among laymen the time has indeed already come when men of
one sort, free and lawful men (*liberi et legales homines*) can be
treated as men of the common, the ordinary, we may perhaps
say the normal sort, while men of all other sorts enjoy privileges
or are subject to disabilities which can be called exceptional. The
lay Englishman, free but not noble, who is of full age and who
has forfeited none of his rights by crime or sin, is the law's
typical man, typical person. But besides such men there are
within the secular order noble men and unfree men; then there
are monks and nuns who are dead to the world; then there is the
clergy constituting a separate "estate"; there are Jews and there
are aliens; there are ex-communicates, outlaws and convicted
felons who have lost some or all of their civil rights; also we may
make here mention of infants and of women, both married and
unmarried, even though their condition be better discussed in
connection with family law, and a word should perhaps be said
of lunatics, idiots, and lepers. Lastly, there are "juristic persons"
to be considered, for the law is beginning to know the corporation. [P. 407]

In the hierarchical structure of the Middle Ages, there
were indeed different statuses. Only a minority of persons
were what Pollock and Maitland call the freeman. Most were
under an umbrella of authority and responsibility like that of
the lord of the manor as described in the quotation from
Marc Bloch which I gave in Chapter 1. As Bloch said, the
manor was a "community of dependents," "by turns protected, commanded, and oppressed by their lord." Priests and
nuns were not persons before the law but were under the
church's umbrella. Women and children were not persons
under the law but were under the umbrella of the husband
and father or male household head. Some were in a marginal
position, with less than full rights, but under no protective
umbrella: Jews, aliens, and convicted felons.

What has happened over the centuries is that one by one,
these status and rights differences have been erased, with only
bare traces of what had been the rigid and hierarchical struc-

ture. The most recent erasures have been in the distinction between men with full rights and women with subordinate rights. The one distinction, however, for which there has been little erasure of status-and-rights differences is the distinction between adults and children. Children find themselves in a social structure of the old type, with their whole person subordinate to another. They, of all persons in society, are least subject to the new form of authority, most subject to the old. This distinction is especially interesting, because the status and rights of children are currently undergoing greatest change. I will not, however, discuss children's rights and children's status in this chapter but will defer that until Chapter 4.

There is, however, in the last sentence of the quotation from Pollock and Maitland, a statement about the status of another kind of person, the juristic person: " ... the law is beginning to know the corporation." Since the thirteenth century, a change has occurred that is of concern to natural persons, not in their own set of statutes before the law, but in the status of this new entity, the "corporation." To show the extent of that change, I will move directly from the thirteenth century to 1982, a time about which Andrew Hacker (1964) has written. His description of the American Electric Company in 1982, a fictional utility company, follows.

By 1972 American Electric had completed its last stages of automation: employees were no longer necessary. Raw materials left on the loading platform were automatically transferred from machine to machine, and the finished products were deposited at the other end of the factory ready for shipment. AE's purchasing, marketing, and general management functions could be handled by ten directors with the occasional help of outside consultants and contractors.

Beginning in 1962 AE's employee pension fund had started investing its capital in AE stock. Gradually it bought more and more of the company's shares on the open market, and by 1968 it was the sole owner of AE. As employees became eligible for retirement—some of them prematurely due to the introduction of automation—the fund naturally liquidated its capital to provide pensions. But instead of reselling its AE shares on the open market, the fund sold the stock to AE itself, which provided the money for pensions out of current income. By 1981 the last AE employee had died, and the pension fund was dissolved. At this time, too, AE became the sole owner of its shares. It had floated no new issues, preferring to engage in self-financing through earnings.

By 1982 the ten directors decided that AE would be well served by the passage of legislation restricting the imports of certain electrical equipment. They therefore secured the services of a public relations firm specializing in political campaigns. The objective was to educate the public and sway grassroots sentiment so that Congress would respond by passing the required bill. The public relations firm was given a retainer of $1 million and told to spend up to $5 million more on advertising and related activities.

Within months the public began to hear about the dire consequences that would follow the importation of alien generators. National security, national prosperity, and the nation's way of life were threatened by a flood of foreign goods. The public relations firm placed several hundred advertisements in newspapers and magazines, and almost a thousand on television. At least fifty citizens' committees "spontaneously" arose to favor the legislation, and over two hundred existing groups passed resolutions in its support. Lectures were given to women's clubs, and films were shown in high schools. By the end of the year—an election year—public sentiment had been aroused and hardly a Congressman was unaware of the popular ferment.

The bill was introduced in both chambers, and a good majority of senators and representatives, abiding by the wishes of their constituents, voted for it. The President signed the bill, and it became law. AE's profits were substantially higher the following year.

A group of senators, however, were curious about what had been going on, and they decided to investigate AE's foray into the political arena. One of the directors was happy to testify, for he knew that no law had been violated. No bribes had been offered, certainly, and no contributions to legislators' campaigns had been made. Toward the end of the inquiry, after all of the techniques employed by the company and the public relations firm had been brought out, the following colloquy took place:

DIRECTOR: . . . And if we undertook these educational and political activities, it was our view that they were dictated by the company's best interests.

SENATOR: Now when you say that these campaigns were on behalf of the "company's" interests, I am not clear what you mean. Were you acting for your stockholders here?

DIRECTOR: I am afraid, Senator, that I cannot say that we were. You see, American Electric has no stockholders. The company owns all its stock itself. We bought up the last of it several years ago.

SENATOR: Well, if not stockholders, then were you acting as a spokesman for American Electric's employees — say, whose jobs might be endangered if foreign competition got too severe?

DIRECTOR: No, sir, I cannot say that either. American Electric is a fully automated company, and we have no employees.

SENATOR: Are you saying that this company of yours is really no more than a gigantic machine? A machine that needs no operators and appears to own itself?

DIRECTOR: I suppose that is one way of putting it. I've never thought much about it.

SENATOR: Then so far as I can see, all of this political pressure that you applied was really in the interests of yourself and your nine fellow directors. You spent almost six million dollars of this company's money pursuing your personal political predilections.

DIRECTOR: I am afraid, Senator, that now I must disagree with you. The ten of us pay ourselves annual salaries of $100,000 year in and year out, and none of us receives any bonuses or raises if profits happen to be higher than usual in a given year. All earnings are ploughed back into the company. We feel very strongly about this. In fact, we look on ourselves as a kind of civil servant. Secondly, I could not say that the decision to get into politics was a pesonal wish on our part. At least eight of the ten of us, as private citizens that is, did not favor the legislation we were supporting. As individuals most of us thought it was wrong, was not in the national interest. But we were acting in the company's interest and in this case we knew that it was the right thing to do.

SENATOR: And by the "company" you don't mean stockholders or employees, because you don't have any . And you don't mean the ten directors because you just seem to be salaried managers which the machine hires to run its affairs. In fact, when this machine gets into politics — or indeed any kind of activity — it has interests of its own which can be quite different from the personal interests of its managers. I am afraid I find all this rather confusing.

DIRECTOR: It may be confusing to you, Senator, but I may say it has been quite straightforward to us at American Electric. We are just doing the job for which we were hired—to look out for the company's interests. [Pp. 3–5]

Although we have reached 1982, there are no companies quite in the position of Hacker's American Electric. But there are many companies that are a long distance on the road from the primitive "juristic person" of the thirteenth century toward American Electric, that is to say, a great many for which action in "the company's interest" is very close to being action in the interest of no natural person.

How did we get from the thirteenth century, when the law was "beginning to know the corporation" to the present, when a scenario like that of the American Electric company is easily conceivable? To answer that question requires an examination of *rights*, since corporate actors have no rights other than those which derive from natural persons; and in this examination it is useful as a first step to review various conceptions throughout history of rights and their origin.

In the new structure of society which contains these large corporate actors detached from natural persons, the distribution of rights and responsibilities among persons and corporate actors is very different from that which existed in the old social structure. And as the new social structure has itself evolved, there have been changes in the distribution of rights and responsibilities. Yet with the extensive, and still increasing, asymmetry between natural persons and corporate actors, it becomes difficult to maintain that balance of rights and that balance of responsibilities among the different kinds of actors which will prove in the end most satisfactory to natural persons.

The conception that a particular balance of rights and a particular balance of responsibilities will prove most satisfactory to natural persons implies that social systems can be evaluated, and that the appropriate criterion of evaluation is how satisfactory they are for natural persons. This will not distinguish evaluatively between all pairs of social systems, for one may be better for some natural persons, and the other better for others. But it does exclude the benefits to corporate actors per se as criteria for evaluation. Corporate actors are intended to serve the ends of natural persons; but fulfillment of their purposes is not in itself a positive value for natural persons. The violation of this principle occurs with some frequency. When vouchers for elementary and secondary education are discussed many persons express concern about "the health of the public schools." And when curtailment of loans for higher education is discussed, many persons (some of whom are the same persons) express concern about the "fate of the private university." Perhaps these expressions of concern implicitly contain the premise that the public school and the private university serve at least some natural persons better than the alternatives (private in one case, public in the other). But if they do not, then the concern implies more interest in the fate of these corporate actors than in the fate of the children and youth they are intended to serve.

To carry out an examination of rights is to do more than merely lay the basis for an examination of the role of corporate actors in modern society. For rights are the basis of authority, and authority is the basis of a social system. Indeed, a useful definition of the extent of a social system is the extent of the body under a governmental authority, that is, under a system of enforced laws. Today, for much of the world, those limits are largely defined by the boundaries of nation-states, for within most nation-states, there is a structure of authority which covers most actions, while between nation-states, the system of international law has only a very limited realm of authority.

Even today, authority in some nation-states is as limited, relative to the realms of authority of subunits within the nation-state, as international law is to that of nation-states. For example, Bedouin tribes in remote desert areas of some nation-states exercise their own internal authority within the tribe, while crimes committed by a member of one tribe against a member of another are settled between tribes according to a principle which makes literal use of the adage,

"An eye for an eye and a tooth for a tooth." That is, punishment by the offended tribe of some member of the offending tribe in precisely the same terms as the original violation: a murder begets a murder, a crippling injury leads to a similar crippling injury, and so on. And in history, similar principles have been widely used among tribes which lived in contiguity but not under a single system of authority. In areas where such principles hold, it is not quite true (because there is not continual and unlimited intertribal war), but almost so, to say that there is anarchy between tribes, and a system of order under some kind of authority within tribes.

In such cases, it is probably most useful to conceive of the social system as not extending beyond the limits of the tribe, because of the near absence of authority transcending the tribal unit. Or more generally, a social system can be seen as consisting of that unit which is covered by a common system of authority, a common system of laws.

THE LOCUS OF SOVEREIGNTY

Authority implies a conception of the locus of ultimate rights or sovereignty, for authority implies that some actors in a system have a legitimate right to control certain actions of others.* This means that within a social system, there is, or comes to be, a belief about the locus of these ultimate rights, and the means by which the rights are transferred to those who actually exercise authoritative control. There have been,

*The term sovereignty unfortunately has had several uses. I am using the term in what is probably its most common use, that is, the ultimate locus of rights to act. Another common usage has to do with the autonomy of authority (rather than action) and is applied most often to "the sovereign state," as a body which is governed by autonomous and encompassing authority, in contrast to nonsovereign associations or other corporate actors subject to the authority of the state, or in contrast to territories such as colonies, which are subject to the authority of an external sovereign state. Laski (1917), for example, uses the term in this latter sense.

in different social systems, widely differing conceptions of the locus of sovereignty. And since the advent of political philosophy, that is, at least since ancient Greece, political philosophers have attempted to capture and express the common conception of the locus of sovereignty as held in the social systems about which they wrote. With the more extensive development of political philosophy beginning in the seventeenth century, political philosophers became somewhat more normatively adventurous, arguing on behalf of conceptions of sovereignty that were not widely held in the social systems of which they were part.

But I will return later to the role of political philosophers in the development of conceptions of sovereignty. At this point, I want merely to describe briefly some of the different conceptions commonly held about the locus of sovereignty in order to locate the conceptions held in various modern social systems. For once we gain a conception of possible loci of ultimate rights, the task of examining the rights held by various natural persons and by various corporate actors, and how we arrived at the present state of society, will become a more straightforward one.

In general, it is possible to say that there has been a long-term evolution from simpler to more complex conceptions of the locus of ultimate rights. An early conception was that of "the divine right of kings." In that conception, found in pre-classical Greece, in ancient Israel, and in ancient Egypt, ultimate authority over all action was held by gods (or in the case of monotheism, by a single god), and was bestowed on a single representative of God, the king. This bestowal occurred in various ways, often concretized in a ceremony with mystical overtones.

This simple and straightforward conception has been throughout history a powerful one. The concept of "charisma" is a conception of a divine gift of extraordinary powers to a single leader, who was then merely the vessel through which these divine powers were exercised. It is likely that the great strength of this conception has been its capacity for bringing a very rapid and extensive vesting of legitimacy in a person, making possible a rapid transformation from anarchy to a system of order.*

The conception of sovereignty based on rights of divine origin vested in the king was, with some modifications, the principal conception in the Holy Roman Empire through Christian Europe, up through the early Middle Ages. There were seen to be two realms of authority, one earthly and the other divine, with two forms of law, civil law and canon law. The king was the holder of earthly power, but he was without full legitimate authority until he received from the pope the bestowal of God's gift of authority and was by that act crowned emperor. There was the imagery, around the eleventh century, of two swords held by the pope, representing authority over matters spiritual and temporal (see Gierke, 1968 [1900]). The pope gave the right to use (though not ownership of) the temporal sword to the king and thus vested in him God's authority over things temporal.

In this conception of divine origins of sovereignty, which effectively located ultimate rights in a single natural person, the king (or emperor), further steps were necessary before actual authority could be exercised, for the king himself could not carry out personally all the actions that were in principle under his authority, nor could he exercise direct authority over more than a few others. In principle, delegation of rights to subordinates, to various corporate actors within his realm (such as extended households, or communities), and to natural persons was necessary, since in principle all actions and all persons were under his authority.

This general conception, that the earthly locus of all authority over action was the king, led naturally to a hierarchical conception of society and of government with all actions being carried out by concession or delegation of authority over the action from the king. It led, in political philosophy, to what is known as "concession theories" of authority within the state

---

*Benjamin Zablocki (1980) in a study of numerous contemporary communes in various states of formation and dissolution, presents evidence that charismatic leadership arises in communes when they are most anarchic, most without a system of legitimate order.

(see Gierke, 1968 [1900]), and to what Walter Ullman has called the "descending" theory of government (Ullman, 1966), in contrast to what may be called the "ascending" theory of government (about which I shall say more shortly). Sovereignty was seen to emanate from the pinnacle of the hierarchy and to be delegated down ("descending") the hierarchy.

In the Middle Ages, during which society was seen as an organic whole, a very different conception of the ultimate locus of rights arose. This was the conception that rights ultimately inhered, not in a single monarch, but as well in the various parts of the natural organic community: the guilds, the villages, the manors, and the individuals themselves. This thesis, which was based on Germanic folk law that had its roots in pre-Christian mores, stood as a competitor to the conception that absolute rights were held by the monarch, who had received them from God through the medium of the pope.*

The conception was more complex than that of the divine right of kings, for there was no single ultimate locus of rights. At the top, at the bottom, and at all intermediate levels, some portion of sovereignty resided. The authority of the king was not complete, nor was there a conception of popular sovereignty. Instead, some authority originated at each point in the rigid hierarchy that constituted the social structure. This was evident in the ritual of homage, in which the man who becomes the vassal kneels and places his hands between those of the man who will be his lord, for in that ritual the man paying homage placed himself under the authority of another. The lord personally held those rights, and if he himself became the vassal of a superior lord, he did not pass on the rights or obligations that he received in the acts of homage of his vassals. There is, in such a ritual, the implicit notion of natural rights, held by the man himself until he paid homage to the man who became his lord.

But the principal contender to the thesis that the ultimate locus of rights was a single central monarch has been, at least

*This thesis is most fully described by Gierke (1934).

since the seventeenth century, that of popular sovereignty: the conception that the ultimate locus of all rights lay in each individual. This thesis of natural rights, however, had to come to grips with the empirical fact that authority was in fact wielded by kings or by a central government apparatus, and that even if existing social systems were not seen as ideal, the very conception of a social system implies a system of authority.

This disparity between the principle of natural rights and the empirical locus of authority was resolved by various political philosophers in various ways, of which I want to select only two for mention: John Locke and Jean-Jacques Rousseau. Locke and Rousseau resolved the problem of how these dispersed individual rights were brought together (or should be, since their theories were partly descriptive and partly normative) in very different ways. Rousseau's conception of the social contract was a conception of a compact among the original holders of rights to give over all individual rights to a "general will." It was necessary for the general will to be administered by a central authority as the agent of the collective. Furthermore, the natural rights given up to the general will included, for Rousseau, the right to withdraw those rights. Once the social contract was made, the general will (and thus its agent, who exercised authority in its name) had absolute authority over those who had joined together to make the social contract.

Locke's conception was that each person had full rights to "life, liberty, and property," and that any authority over his actions which he gave up he could revoke at any time. That is, each person gave up only the *right to use* certain rights, for the rights themselves were seen as inalienable. Thus Locke had a conception of a social contract, but one that, in contrast to Rousseau's, covered only a fraction of his rights and was at any time revocable. Representative government, with the representatives responsible to their constituents, was the instrument by which that authority necessary to maintain order was exercised.

The conception held in liberal democracies as well as in socialist states of the ultimate locus of rights is that of popular sovereignty: rights inhere in each natural person. In both these forms of modern states, in contrast to ancient forms, governments are seen to obtain both their power and legitimacy from the transfer of individual rights to the government. This is what Walter Ullman terms the "ascending theory" of government, for the ultimate loci of rights are the separate individuals, and the transfer of these rights constitutes an ascension of rights from multiple sovereigns to the few who will exercise authority. The central difference between liberal democracies and socialist states in political philosophy is that between Locke and Rousseau: in liberal democracies, the transfer of rights is seen to be partial and revocable, and political institutions are established to insure that the principle of revocability is met in practice; in socialist states, the transfer of rights is seen to be total and nonrevocable, with the principal aim of insuring that all economic resources are owned by the state (i.e., by the people collectively), so that no person can engage in economic exploitation of another.*

*The USSR constitution includes, in Articles 118–129, a list of the "fundamental rights of citizens." While some of these rights are rights to claim certain benefits from the state (the right to education, old-age security, medical service, paid labor), others are the sort of liberties of which natural rights are ordinarily seen to consist: freedom of worship, freedom of speech, freedom of the press, freedom of assembly and meetings, freedom of street processions and demonstrations, freedom to organize, to have privacy of correspondence, and to be free from arbitrary arrest (Berman and Quigley, 1969). From the constitution it would appear that the USSR has more the character of a Lockean than a Rousseauean social contract. However, the lack of enabling institutions to insure that these rights are secure suggests that the constitutional provisions are there primarily to provide grounds for the claim that fundamental liberties ("natural rights" or "human rights") are not violated in the Soviet Union. Yet their very presence indicates the power of the natural rights conception.

It is interesting to speculate about the extraordinary difference between the kinds of governmental systems established by these two philosophers. Rousseau was no totalitarian; he would never have assented to a state formed along the lines of his theory of social contract, had he seen its totalitarian consequences. Yet he never conceived of any institution which would prevent those consequences by protecting the individual from the state, acting in the name of the people. Rousseau's life, as well as his general approach to politi-

Thus the dominant conception of the ultimate locus of rights in modern nation-states is the conception that they inhere in natural persons individually. A signal of the universality of this conception in modern nation-states is the universality of popular elections. Even when, as in one-party states, popular election provides no de facto popular control, election symbolizes the transfer by electors of certain individual rights to the elected. These rights consist, in effect, of the "usage rights" of sovereignty, that is, the right to exercise authority, constrained only by the limits imposed by the constitution.

Thus for the single exceptional corporate actor in modern society, that is, the state, there is a general consensus, shared in both liberal democracies and socialist states, that the ultimate locus of all rights is the individual, and the state obtains its rights by a voluntary transfer by individuals of those rights. There is, however, less consensus on the origin of rights held by corporate actors other than the state. Do they receive their rights, as does the state, from individuals, the original loci of the rights? Or do they receive their rights at a second remove, from the state which has received the rights from their original owners?

---

cal philosophy, were vastly different from Locke's. Locke was involved in politics, spent time in exile in Holland, and helped to bring about the accession of William of Orange to the throne after the death of Charles II. His writings had an empirical concreteness, possibly derived from his political experience. Rousseau's life, in contrast, was ascetic and removed from practical affairs; and his writings were characterized by a kind of abstract idealism which was quite removed from concrete political practice. It is quite possible that his innocence of the practice of politics blinded him to the necessity of going beyond an abstract conception of the "general will" to the institutions which would realize the aims he desired. (Of course, had he tried to do so, he would have found this impossible without revising his conception of the social contract, because in the transfer of all natural rights to the general will, individuals were left with no weapons to protect themselves from arbitrary exercise of those rights against them.)

THE ACQUISITION OF RIGHTS BY CORPORATE ACTORS

For the socialist state, based on Rousseau's conception of all rights amalgamated into the general will at the disposal of the central organs of the state, the path through which corporate actors acquire rights is clear. Any dispensation of rights to corporate actors *within* the state, or even to natural persons, must come from the state itself. Thus all purposive corporate actors within the social system exist only by the leave of the people collectively, that is, by the leave of the agent of the general will, the central state government. The rights of any subordinate corporate actor, obtained through delegation from the central organ, are defined and circumscribed by that organ. With few exceptions, which are ordinarily seen as harmless to the state,* the corporate actor becomes a subordinate agent of the state, for it does not exist independently of the state. If a trade union, it exists as an organ of the state; if a business firm, it exists as a different organ of the state. The organizational structure of the society becomes one that is very much like the hierarchical structure of the Middle Ages, with each corporate entity occupying a particular, well-defined position within that hierarchical structure.† The principle of delegation of state authority to the different organs which constitute the corporate actors of the society follows the "concession theory" by which corporate bodies were established. In the shift away from the hierarchical social structure of the Middle Ages, the first stage of that shift involved the possibility of new corporate actors coming into existence, but only through a concession from the king or the

---

*One exception in Poland throughout its socialist history has been the Polish Sociological Association, an indication of the lack of concern of state authorities about the potential dangers of sociologists.

†The structure differs from the hierarchy of the Middle Ages, however, in that subordinate actors within the structure derive their authority wholly from that of the state, while each had sovereign rights in the political structure of the Middle Ages.

state.* In Russia, where capitalism developed later than in Central and Western Europe, and thus where the demand for creation of autonomous corporate actors was slower in arriving, the principle of corporate actors receiving rights only through concession from the czar was never replaced by more liberal conditions, and that principle was in effect taken over and strengthened by the Soviet Union when it was formed. "Concession" is in fact too weak a word, for it implies grant of freedom to act independently of the authority of the state, while the corporate actors established in socialist states are extensions of the state or agents of the state, acting under the authority of the central organ of the state to carry out purposes of the state.

In liberal democracies, the answer to the origin of corporate actors' rights is less clear. Do corporate actors themselves have natural rights, do their rights come from natural persons

---

*The difference between concession and autonomous corporate actors can be exemplified by two methods through which gasoline stations and restaurants came into existence along interstate highways in the United States. On toll roads there are "service areas" at intervals, containing gasoline stations and restaurants. These are established by concession from the state which owns the toll road. On nontoll interstate highways there are exits to access roads, and at many of these exits gasoline stations and restaurants have been established without concession from the state, by purchase of land from farmers whose land borders the highway and by construction of a gasoline station or restaurant or both on that land. In the case of the toll highways with concessions, there is initial competition in bids for the concession but subsequently an absence of competition. In the case of the nontoll interstate highways, there is continuing competition. (It is true that some competition for the concessions arises from the less conveniently located stations and restaurants outside the toll road perimeters. This by definition does not exist in a social system in which all corporate bodies operate through concession. It is also true that in a system with external competition outside the toll road, competition could be induced within the toll road through a different use of the power of concession. For example, alternate service areas could be conceded to different concession operators. It is instructive, however, to see that this seldom occurs, though it would be to the interest of toll road users — mostly natural persons — for it to occur. Its near absence is likely due to collusion between two corporate actors, the state and the concessionaires, or to collusion in which agents of the state receive personal benefits from the concessionaires.)

as individuals directly, or are the rights received through concession from the people collectively, that is, from the state? In all nation-states, both profit-making and non-profit corporations must be chartered (though in the United States, chartering is done by the states rather than by the national government). This would appear to follow the concession theory. However, for two reasons, the requirement for chartering has less force than it would seem. First, the charter consists of a large measure of liberties, ordinarily limited only, as are natural persons, by the laws of the state. Second, the evolution of common law in the courts has presumed, in the absence of reasons to the contrary, the corporate actors have the status of persons. Thus rights of natural persons protected by the Constitution are also presumed to be the rights of corporate actors. For example, the Fourteenth Amendment on equal protection, initially passed to protect the rights of freed slaves, was used widely by corporations in the decades following its enactment.

Even freer from the state's authority is an invention which arose in Lombardy, was picked up in England to facilitate the transfer of real property between generations, and then became widely used in England and (especially) the United States in the late nineteenth and early twentieth centuries: the trust. A trust required no charter from the state and could hold assets corporately, while avoiding the designation of *persona ficta,* and thus avoiding the responsibilities and obligations which corporations had. For example, an early use of the trust was by nonconformist churches in England. Members of nonconformist churches feared the necessity to be chartered by the state, because of control by the Church of England which could be used to prevent their being chartered. This would prevent those churches from holding property (such as the church building) apart from the individuals who made them up (whose property was of course subject to inheritance taxes). Members of these churches were able to circumvent this by the trust, a device which had only recently come into use in England. With the trust they placed the church's resources in the hands of a set of trustees, thus protecting them from the state and the Church of England (see Maitland, 1904).

Because of the special position of sovereignty, or suzerainty, of the state, it is perhaps conceptually more accurate to say that all other corporate actors in liberal democracies gain their rights and resources through a combination of two routes: one route is directly from those individuals who combine resources to create the corporate actor and vest in it a portion of their natural rights; the other is indirectly through the state which grants a charter, giving the corporate actor rights to certain kinds of actions. It is the combination of rights and resources obtained through these two routes that breathes a corporate life into this intangible actor.

I have dwelt at length on some aspects of political philosophy, for it is important to begin from a point of conceptual clarity when we ask the next question: what has gone wrong? Why does it often appear that corporate actors such as large business corporations or large trade unions have gained excessive rights, while natural persons are helpless in their interactions with these corporate actors? Why does it often appear that the state has aggrandized its power at the expense of its citizens? If all rights inhere in natural persons individually, why do these corporate actors, from the state on down, often appear to have captured the principal rights in modern society, and left natural persons like you and me as dependent on them, and as subject to their whim, as the vassal of the Middle Ages who had given himself over to a lord's protection, or even perhaps of the serf who was wholly subject to the will of his lord?

If the institution of the trust served as a way for natural persons who were religious nonconformists in England to defend themselves against the oppression of the Church of England and the state, how does it happen that "trust-busting" and the Sherman Anti-Trust Act came to be seen as a necessary defense of natural persons against corporations? If the liberty to combine resources to engage in joint enterprise helped free persons from fixed states, circumscribed rights, and unalterable futures, then how is it that this same joint enterprise, in the form of large corporations, can constrain the rights of natural persons with whom they interact — whether employees or customers? If the institution of trade

unions, and the rights given to trade unions by the Wagner
Act, served as a way of rescuing rights of workers from powerful employers, why is it that there comes into being a National Right to Work Committee, which uses the courts to
protect natural persons against the unions of which they are
members? If the liberal state served as the vehicle by which
persons could be free from subordination and dependence,
how is it that this same state can be seen as oppressive and the
principal source of erosion of natural persons' rights? It is
interesting that for the first time in history as far as I know,
the strongest ideological positions, from the new left to the
neoconservatives to the new right, contain as a central element hostility to corporate actors in their current forms, including in all cases the state. The neoconservative and new
right ideology is directed wholly against the power of the
state; and the new left ideology, unlike the old Stalinist left,
includes the "giant bureaucracy" of the state as a target of its
hostility along with the "giant corporation."

FOUR STRUCTURES FOR THE FLOW OF RIGHTS

Perhaps it is useful, before going further, to see dia-
grammatically the essential differences among the four structures through which I have described sovereignty as seen to
originate and to be delegated. The four structures I will call
the divine right of kings, Genossenschaftstheorie, state
socialism, and pluralist democracy. In the divine right of
kings, shown in Figure 2.1 (a), sovereignty originates at the
top of a hierarchy, and for purposes of governing, parts of
those rights are delegated down the hierarchy.

    In Figure 2.1 (b), Genossenschaftstheorie, which had its
origins in Central European folkways in the Middle Ages, and
was expressed in natural law, there is also a hierarchy but with
sovereignty originating at each level and transmitted upward.
At each level of the hierarchy is a social unit, such as the
manor or the guild or the village, and some portion of the
total sovereignty in society was seen as originating at each of

FIGURE 2.1

Origins and Destinations of Rights in Four Types of Political Systems

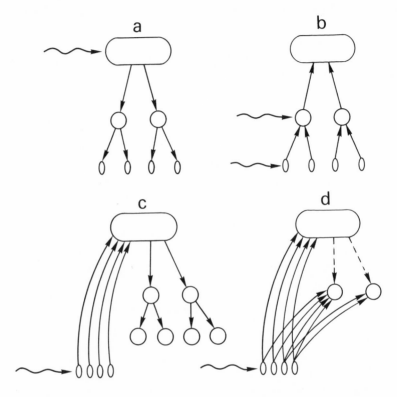

these points. Ceremonies like the ceremony of homage which I referred to earlier symbolized the upward transmission of sovereignty. The result was a social structure that was no less hierarchical than that of the structure in diagram (a), but one in which the rights could in principle be revoked at various points in the hierarchy — so that we could say that residual rights remained distributed through the structure.

In Figure 2.1 (c), state socialism, all sovereignty originates with natural persons individually, and all is transmitted upward to the central state apparatus. Then, for purposes of governing, parts of those rights are, as in structure (a), delegated down to subordinate corporate actors which in effect become agents of the state. In Poland, Hotel Europejski, where the waitress of Episode 2 in Chapter 1 works, is not an autonomous corporate actor but an agent of the State Tourist Agency, Orbis, which itself is an agency of the state. It is for this reason that the alternate scenario I described, in which the waitress was acting not only as the agent of the Hotel Europejski, but also of the state, is less outrageous than it might otherwise be — for as an agent of the hotel she was already indirectly an agent of the state.

In effect, this structure is hierarchical in much the same form as the monarchical structure of (a), containing only the additional component of the initial collection of sovereignty from individuals to the central source.

In Figure 2.1 (d), pluralist democracy, sovereignty originates, as in (c), with natural persons individually. But here only a portion is transmitted to the state as corporate actor; part continues to be held individually and part is transmitted to other corporate actors, the "intermediate institutions" of a pluralist political system. Yet these corporate actors require, in order to exist, some acquiescence from the "collectivized" portion of individual sovereignty, that is, the state apparatus. This is the purpose of the broken lines going downward from the top of the hierarchy to the intermediate corporate actors. The broken lines symbolize something less than the full hierarchical authority found in (a) and (c). The sense in which such a structure can be regarded as pluralistic is the fact that a portion of the original sovereignty never passes into the hands of the state but is lodged directly in the other corporate actors, which can then be said to have a measure of authority independent of state authority.

This partial transmission of sovereignty to the state in pluralist democracies makes it the most complex system of the four outlined in Figure 2.1. This complexity has led to confusion among legal theorists in such states looking for the locus of sovereignty from which authority emanates. For example, the legal positivists, perhaps best represented by H. L. A. Hart (1961) or earlier by John Austin (1954 [1879]) embark on a search for the ultimate locus of sovereignty which gives the authority to establish laws, and often stop at the central legislative body, the Parliament or Congress (although sometimes they go the step further as does Hart [1961, p. 70] to the electors of the legislature, that is, to popular sovereignty).

Their conception of the law is as a unidirectional exercise of authority, leading them naturally to look for a hierarchy with an apex from which the commands flow. This, of course, suggests far more the monarchical structure (a) or the socialist state (c).

Another set of legal theorists, however, exemplified by Lon L. Fuller (1969), sees the law more nearly as a compact between those who establish the laws and the general population covered by the laws. Fuller's conception of the law is less as a set of commands than as a set of rules governing interactions among the population. Friedrich Hayek (1973) shares this latter conception, seeing the conception of law as held by the legal positivists as comparable to authority in an *organization*, of which the most common form is that with an internal hierarchical structure like (a) in Figure 2.1, in contrast to laws which establish a *just order* in a society.

This confusion and disagreement among legal theorists and political philosophers is not, of course, unrelated to the power that they envisage as appropriate for the state; those who see the authority on which laws are based as unidirectional, and the laws themselves as authoritative commands, are more likely to be those who see a more activist and powerful government as proper in a pluralist democracy. Those who see the law as a social compact, with sovereignty resting in no central set of law makers, are more likely to be those who see the proper role of the central government as embodying little power, and acting in primarily adjudicative ways.

The disagreements themselves illustrate the point that what is labelled "pluralist democracy" in this discussion is not a single distribution of rights but is a whole continuum, ranging from a very small fraction of rights transmitted to the state as corporate actor (approaching an anarchical form, in which all rights are held individually) to a very large fraction of rights transmitted to the state, approaching a state-socialist or Rousseauean form.

TRANSFORMATION FROM ONE STRUCTURE
TO ANOTHER

A question of some practical as well as theoretical importance is the question of whether there are processes through which any of these structures can come to be transformed to others. In particular, it is sometimes believed that there are processes within pluralist democracies which tend to transform them into socialist systems—not through the accession to power of a socialist political party but rather through some natural processes that operate independently of conscious ideology. And conversely, it is sometimes believed that there are processes within state socialist systems which tend to transform them into systems not greatly different from pluralist democracies. If there are processes of one or the other of these two kinds, we may find that we are confronted with a still newer social structure than the one we inhabit, yet not one of our own choice. Consequently, it is important to discover if there are such processes. This takes us directly back to rights, and to the possibility that certain rights, ordinarily seen as indivisible, can in fact be separated.

THE SEPARATION OF BENEFIT RIGHTS
AND USAGE RIGHTS

What is ordinarily thought of as "ownership" of a resource or a right can be fragmented into various parts. Only in some social systems are the various rights which constitute what we think of as the rights of ownership in fact bundled together. They are, in fact, sometimes separated out even in those systems in which "ownership" is recognized. For example, in many cities in the United States, if a person owns a house which has been designated a historic landmark, he cannot alter this house without approval from city officials. One of the elements in the package of ownership rights has been removed. Or in the Middle Ages in Europe, what we now call ownership of land was divided into several rights:

the right to the land burdens or taxes, the right to use of the land, the right to pass it on to heirs (see Denman, 1958). Or in some Bedouin tribes, various components of ownership rights to a camel are neatly separated out. One person has milking rights; another has riding rights; another has, if the camel is killed, rights to the camel meat, and still another rights to the skin. There is, in short, no such thing as a single "right of ownership" to a camel in those tribes.

Like rights over a camel in these Bedouin tribes, ownership of a resource or a right has come to be divided in modern society into different components. Ordinarily there are two major components which are separated out, which can be called "usage rights" and "benefit rights." It is perhaps easiest to see how this separation occurs not at the level of the state as a corporate actor but for corporate actors within the state. It is here that the separation of these two rights has been most fully studied.

One context within which this separation has been examined at length is that of business corporations. Adolph Berle and Gardiner Means (1940) carried out the groundbreaking study of this in the 1930s. Berle and Means suggested that the modern corporation in the United States has "split the atom of private property" into what they termed "active property" and "passive property." What they meant was that private property consisted of two rights: the right to control the use of that property for the pursuit of a given purpose, and the right to benefit from the use of the property. They showed how, in the modern American public corporation, the managers of the corporation held the usage rights, that is, the power to determine the specific uses of the corporation's wealth, while the owners retained the right to benefit from that use, through dividends and interest, as well as the right of ultimate disposal, bringing the benefits of capital gains. What I have termed "usage rights" and what Berle and Means term "active property" is the right to determine use of the corporate resources. It is this right which in many corporate actors is constitutionally dispersed among many members or owners, with each having some voice (ordinarily through voting but also through other rights, such as the right to speak in a union meeting or a stockholders' meeting) in the direction of the organization. But Berle and Means have shown that despite such constitutional rights in the modern corporation, the effective voice of the original owners is very small.

This is, of course, as it must be, for if stockholders' rights to control the corporation's direction were continually exercised, the corporation would act in a less consistent and purposeful way; or if the union members' rights to control the union's direction were continually exercised, the union would be unable to act consistently and with strength. Under many conditions, those who constitutionally hold rights to affect the direction of the corporate actor's action fail to do so, because they trust the actions of the central executives in direct control of the resources. But what Berle and Means found in addition was that the original owners had also given up a considerable part of their ability to revoke those usage rights if they no longer trusted the central executives. And with that loss came another: loss of the ability to protect their benefit rights. The central executives, freed from the potential power of the owners to remove them, were free to use the resources of the corporate actor for other ends, including their own personal ends.

A similar process has been shown by various authors in the case of voluntary associations and trade unions. In principle, the members have a voice in determining corporate action, but in practice, the voice is ineffective and the corporate body is controlled by its managers. Robert Michels (1949) showed how this is true in a normatively democratic organization, the German Social Democratic Party, and expressed this fact in his "iron law of oligarchy," as a general principle applicable to all large organizations with broad membership. The applicability to trade unions with an oligarchic central administration and a dispersed membership was shown by S. M. Lipset et al. (1956) by examination of a deviant case, the International Typographical Union, in which members *did* have a voice in determining union action. In these corporate actors, as in the modern corporation, not only has the right to use a set of rights and resources been given up to the central executives; in addition, with the exception of deviant cases, there has been an inadvertent loss of the right to revoke that usage from the central executive. The result is that the central executive is no longer constrained in his use of the corporate resources but can employ them to his own end, or to other ends not coincident with those of the original owners of the resources. The results of this process are perhaps most often seen in the case of union leaders who are found to have diverted union funds for their own benefits. But even where no illegal actions have been taken, the corporate actor's resources are frequently drained off to provide special benefits to those in immediate control of them. What is striking is the similarity between organizations that are opposed by interest and often by ideology, that is, business corporations and trade unions. In both, those in control of the organization's resources are able to benefit at the expense of those who are the ultimate sovereigns. And in both, those in control accomplish the task by using their control of the organization's resources to benefit themselves.

Similar processes occur at the level of the state as a corporate actor. Through the representative process persons give up large amounts of sovereignty in order to achieve ends that they see as collective benefits. In this way they lose direct control of extensive resources and trust to their mechanisms of representative government and to the occupants of government positions to exercise that control in ways they desire. But the analysis of Michels and Berle and Means hold here as well: those resources, given over to government, deprive persons of control over their employ, giving that control largely to the corporate agencies of government, which are partly insulated from control by persons from whom those resources came.

Those who come into direct control of those resources are then freed to use them for their own personal ends, or toward other goals that do not coincide with those of the citizen-sovereigns. In the events in Poland following August 1980, a general phenomenon which suddenly came to light was the illegal use of collective resources by local authorities and managers of industry to build luxurious villas for themselves.

And a general pattern of collusive arrangements in which officials at all levels received special benefits (such as state-subsidized apartments) was discovered.

The general process can be described as one in which the holders of usage rights to resources can employ those rights to bring about ends which do not coincide with the ends of the nominal owners of those rights. In this way the corporate actors of society come to be increasingly freed from constraints by natural persons and capable of pursuing directions chosen by those who control them.

The consequence of this process for the structure of state socialism, Figure 2.1 (c), is to remove effective control from the original sovereigns, thus making the structure (c) more like that of (a) or (b). That is, although the original sovereignty was seen to be in the hands of natural persons, the effect of this process is to create a structure in which sovereignty effectively lies in the hands of the central state authority. The structure of authority becomes in effect a wholly hierarchical one.

The same general tendencies are present in structure (d), the pluralist democracy. That is, those who hold the usage rights to sovereignty, the central state authorities, come to be freed from the original sovereigns. But there is an impediment. The principal impediment arises from the fact that the process by which the central authority frees itself from the individuals who give it that authority depends on their fragmentation and dispersion. If they have combined other resources in corporate actors independent of the state, then this fragmentation and dispersion no longer holds. And this is precisely the character of a pluralist democracy: there are other corporate actors, relatively independent of the state, which may be used to oppose the power that has been brought together in the hands of the central state apparatus. The corporate actors that can be used for such purposes include all kinds: business corporations, trade unions, voluntary associations, churches. The principal element necessary is independence from the superordinate corporate actor, the state.

In asking whether there are processes through which one

structure is transformed to another, I will turn first to processes within structure, (c), Figure 2.1, socialism, which tend to transform it into a pluralist structure, (d).

THE DRIFT OF POWER TO THE USER
IN THE SOCIALIST STATE

There is, at the same time as the processes I have just described, another process which tends to give structures (a) and (c) some of the characteristics of (d), a pluralist democracy. The process is an extension of the separation of usage rights from benefit rights.

Corporate actors are intangible bodies; consequently, they must employ persons as agents to use the resources vested in them. Whether these agents are corporation executives and employees, union officials and employees, government officials and employees, or still another form of agent, the corporate body must place in their hands usage rights to the resources.

In vesting these usage rights in persons who act as its agents, corporate actors give power to these persons. The persons, in turn, may use this power to divert some of the benefits to themselves. If a personnel officer in a firm has some discretion in hiring, he may use that discretion to hire his friends or to create obligations to him. If a government official has information about a policy involving land acquisition, he may use that information to benefit himself, directly or indirectly. If a union official has the power to negotiate a wage contract, he may use it to gain entrance to the country club. If a worker has the right to use a set of tools or a salesman the right to use an automobile, the tools or automobile may be used to serve personal ends as well. If an employee has use of an expense account, he may well use it to his own benefit.

All these activities stem from the necessity of a corporate body to deploy its resources in the hands of persons who occupy positions within it; and although some personal uses of these resources are preventable, others are not, without immobilizing the organization. And even without the illegal or questionable actions which use corporate resources for private gain, there are ways that a person's position in a corporate actor benefit him. He has credit references for loans and credit cards, and he has in effect a co-insurer for many activities, as evidenced by the frequency of the question, "Who do you work for?" as a means of establishing a person's trustworthiness. In addition, a worker gains certain rights to his job over a period of time, a little comparable to squatter's rights, codified in seniority rights and rights of protection against summary dismissal.

The process is exactly the same as that which gives a corporate actor power in the first place: the drift of power to those who actually engage in the use of resources and away from those who have ultimate rights of ownership of these resources. This drift describes both the gain in power of managers relative to owners or members, as described by Berle and Means and by Michels, and the gain in power of those persons in organizational positions to which resources of the organizations have been delegated.

This appropriation of corporate resources by those in direct control of them (that is, those agents to whom control over these resources has been delegated) appears particularly extensive in socialist systems. For example, it is estimated that a significant percentage of the total productive activity in the Soviet Union involves state resources diverted for private use.

But not only is it the case that agents can use the resources of the corporate actor to benefit themselves individually; those resources can sometimes be used to create a corporate actor that can represent the interests of natural persons in opposition to those of the corporate actor.

Two examples, which at first appear different, but are in fact quite similar, illustrate this: first, the organizational potential resulting from continued association of persons with common interests has led workers in capitalist corporations to form unions to represent their interests. The resources for organization were inadvertently provided by the corporation itself, through the physical contiguity it brought about. Second, the organizational potential resulting from continued association of persons with common interests led workers in socialist Poland to form an independent union, Solidarity. It is in part, of course, a different set of organizational resources which has provided the base for Solidarity, and these should not be overlooked. These are the resources of the Catholic church, the one important corporate actor which has not been an agent of the state but has been fully independent.* But in part also it has been the resources provided by the state itself: the organizational potential of young workers working in a large workplace and associating with others of their own age and with similar life chances; and the human capital that the state provides through the educational system.†

Such resources as these make possible a further extension of the process by which usage rights over resources can enable their holders to oppose the interests of the actor who has delegated these rights. In the process as discussed earlier, this autonomous power arose when usage rights (or Berle and Means's "active property") were being concentrated for use by the state or another corporate actor; here, autonomous power arises when these usage rights are further delegated to the agents. The principles behind Robert Michels' iron law of oligarchy operate in the decentralized deployment of resources as well as in the initial concentration of resources at the central executive: the unit comes to take on interests of its own and to use the resources at its disposal to further those interests.

For this reason, in hierarchical systems, such as that in Figure 2.1 (c), in which sovereignty has come to be held at the

---

*For example, the leaders of Solidarity are practicing Catholics; and the Catholic militia which kept order during the visit of the Polish pope constituted a cadre which was important in the organization and discipline of the Solidarity movement. Although church officials (e.g. Cardinal Wishinski) have not always stood solidly behind the workers' movement, the organizational resources provided by the church have been important to the movement.

†The importance of the workplace as a locus for association is illustrated by the Polish military government's action after the imposition of martial law in December 1981. All gatherings but those of religious services were banned; and in order to keep shipyard workers dispersed, they were ordered not to report to work.

top, the drift of power to the actor who holds usage rights not only in the first instance concentrates power at the top; the same process, because of the necessity to deploy resources through agents, can lead to power and autonomy in the hands of those agents. The interests of these various subordinate corporate actors and persons differ, as in a pluralistic structure, and each of these actors can make use of the resources at its disposal to pursue its interests—in somewhat the same way that occurs in a system that is explicitly pluralist.

THE INCREASING SUBORDINATION OF CORPORATE ACTORS TO THE STATE IN PLURALIST STATES

There is also a process in pluralist democracies that increases the concentration of power in the state. This is the very use of the state apparatus as described earlier to rebalance the rights of persons and corporate actors in type-2 relations. The constraints imposed on rights of corporate actors, while supported by natural persons, and sometimes initiated by them through their elected representatives, often take the form of closer supervision by the state. For example, to insure nondiscrimination in employment decisions of corporate actors, an Equal Employment Opportunity Commission is created, *as an agency of the central state apparatus.* Or to insure safety of certain consumer products, a Food and Drug Administration is created, again as an agent of the central state apparatus.

The effect of such extensions of the state governing apparatus is to put the independent corporate actors more nearly under control of the central state authority. In the diagram (d), the effect is to fill in the broken lines, to make solid lines putting the corporate actors under the authority of the state.

A second set of actions of the state, made in the interests of natural persons, acts further to place the independent corporate actors—whether business corporations, trade unions, or voluntary associations—under the authority of the state. I indicated earlier that a major difference between the old social structure and the new is the fact that the corporate actors in the new social structure had no authority over, nor responsibility for, persons. The fundamental change in structure had replaced responsibility for persons with responsibility for actions, as part of the same structural change in which persons as elements of the organizational structure were replaced by positions.

This, however, has had the consequence not only of freeing persons from the authority of medieval corporate actors, but also of leaving no actors responsible for them as persons, beyond their immediate families. To counter this, there has come to be an increasing demand that some corporate actor take that responsibility. The demand has been acted upon by the state in two ways. The first is by an increasing paternalism of the state itself, in the form of the welfare state. The second is through legislation which imposes on modern corporate actors some of the responsibility for the person which was characteristic of the manor. This legislation requires corporate actors to provide certain benefits for employees, making them increasingly responsible for the person as a whole. Such areas of benefits as unemployment compensation, pensions, health care, freedom from arbitrary dismissal, and others have begun to become part of the corporate actor's responsibility, to be enforced by agencies of the central state apparatus. Again this strengthens the lines of authority from the state to the corporate actor. This can be seen by the parallels between the emerging state-imposed paternalism of these corporate actors and constitutionally determined paternalism of corporate actors in state socialism. Those subordinate corporate actors, such as industrial enterprises, assume some responsibility not only for activities but for persons as well. For example, in the constitution of the USSR, among the "fundamental rights of citizens" are listed not only the fundamental liberties that are ordinarily seen as civil liberties; listed as well are the following rights (Berman and Quigley, 1969):

Article 118: The right to a guaranteed job with payment.
Article 119: The right to rest and leisure: annual paid vacations, sanatoria, rest homes, and clubs for workers.

Article 120: Old age security, free medical service, health resorts
for workers.
Article 121: The right to education.

These rights are responsibilities assumed by the state and its
subordinate agencies for the person as a whole. They are not
different in kind, however, from the emerging responsibilities
for persons imposed on corporate actors in the pluralist state.

The problem, from the point of view of the interests of
natural persons, is that both these processes—the direct constraints on rights of corporate actors, and the state-imposed
requirements for paternalism on the part of corporate actors
—in strengthening the authority link from the state to those
corporate actors within the state's scope of sovereignty, reduce
the possibility that these actors can prevent the state from
aggrandizing its power and insulating itself from the natural
persons in whom sovereignty originally resided. Yet both of
these processes are initated to aid and protect the interests of
natural persons. What is necessary to ask is whether those
interests can be protected by means which do not strengthen
the power of the state.

REMEDIES FOR CORPORATE ACTORS

What kinds of interventions of the state in the relations between persons and corporate actors will *not* have the defects
of power aggrandizement to the state which I have described?
And what kinds of internal modifications of those actors
themselves will make them more satisfactory as fellow inhabitants of the modern social structure? Let me address the
first question first. The use of the state as protector and agent
of natural persons, by supervising and regulating the actions
of the corporate actor, has an extraordinarily serious defect:
as intended it reduces the imbalance in rights between natural
persons and one set of corporate actors; but by increasing the
set of powers held collectively by the state, it increases the
imbalance in rights between natural persons and the state.

Corporate actors other than the state grow weaker, and lose some of their autonomy; but that power does not merely vanish, nor does it go to natural persons individually. It goes somewhere, and that is to the state as the protector of natural persons.

There is a wholly different strategy of state intervention which is sometimes used and which does not have this defect. This is to modify the rules governing the particular relation between persons and corporate actors in such a way that the effects of the asymmetry are overcome. For example, OSHA functions through government regulations about safety conditions in the work place. An alternative law, which exemplifies the different strategy, would have been one which gave workers increased rights in determining the safety conditions under which they work—either through their existing collective bargaining organizations, or through something like the co-determination law which recently became effective in Germany.

The co-determination law in effect writes a new charter for German profit-making corporations, one in which stockholders have fewer rights in determining corporate action. This change occurs at two levels: at the board of directors level of large firms ten of twenty-one board members are representatives of stockholders and ten are representatives of employees. At the shop floor level there are worker councils, which have authority over many issues affecting workers' conditions.

To express the difference between this and laws like OSHA: in this case, there is a one-time intervention of the state to augment the rights of employees of a corporation. Employees are given, by this intervention, a tool with which to protect their own interests. Their power is increased, but that of the state is not appreciably increased. In contrast, a law like that which created OSHA makes the nation-state the protector—and like the lord of the manor, this increases the state's ability to "by turns protect, command and oppress." Similar to the German co-determination law was the Wagner Act in the United States, passed in 1936. This act changed the rules of the game, giving more rights to workers and reducing the rights of the corporate actors which employed them, but not greatly increasing the power of the state.

If this strategy in which the state is a rule setter, establishing rules of the game which give more rights to natural persons, is superior to the state-as-protector strategy, why is it not always used? I think the answer is in the fact that it does not provide certainty—and that legislators or officials of government agencies prefer to gain control over the outcome rather than to let it be determined by the parties directly involved. This indicates further, if I am correct, the danger of such laws — for they place more authority in the hands of the most powerful corporate actor of all, the state.

Yet laws which change the rules of the game, rather than "protector laws," are easier for some types of rights than others. They are easiest for OSHA-type rights, involving natural persons as employees, more difficult for FDA-type rights, involving natural persons as customers, and most difficult for EPA-type rights, involving the rights of natural persons who are "third parties"—who have no explicit relation to the corporate actor but are indirectly affected by its actions. The differential difficulty arises from the differential degree of organization, or ease of organization, of employees, customers, and third parties. I will not dwell on the difficulties here but will return to them in the last chapter in the discussion of one component of those rights, "information rights."

Rather, I want now to turn to a slightly different question: what kind of changes, other than those imposed by the state, might corporate actors below the state level undergo, wholly in their own interest, which would make them more satisfactory components of the social structure we inhabit? For example, Japanese firms seem to function better in some ways as organizations than do American firms. They are also organized differently. Does this different mode of organization make them more satisfactory for those persons who interact with them as employees or as customers?

A beginning view of the general question can be obtained by looking again at the diagrams. Applying these diagrams now not to the state, but to corporate actors within the state, which of the four structures is most like that of a corporation

— or for that matter, of a trade union? The answer is (c). A large capitalist firm is — paradoxically — internally organized in a way closest to that of state socialism.

In place of citizens with natural rights, there are in a business corporation stockholders with capital; or in a union, there are union members with their bargaining rights and their dues. In place of the government bureaucracy is the company bureaucracy, or the bureaucracy of union officials. And certainly, as Adolph Berle and Gardiner Means discovered for corporations, and as Robert Michels discovered for trade unions, there is the process which gives autonomous power to those in control of the bureaucracy. In neither of these types of corporate actors is there an institutional structure to insure that the original sovereigns retain power. Rather, in both cases, the structure is hierarchical, of form (c) in Figure 2.1.

What kinds of internal structural changes might these corporate actors undergo, to overcome the defects of this structure?

I will not answer this question at this point but will defer it until after examining another aspect of the new social structure: the risks imposed on natural persons by actions of corporate actors. Then we will be in a position to return, in the latter part of that chapter, to the question of internal changes within corporate actors.

DIALOGUE 2

Q: Your argument, I believe, is internally inconsistent. You first claim that the essential difference between state socialism and pluralist democracy is that natural persons in the latter reserve some of their rights to be vested in intermediate corporate actors, which are then able to counter the power of the state. But then you tell me that these intermediate corporate actors are themselves organized like state socialism and take control away from the natural persons who have vested authority in them. By your own argument, then, natural persons have no more control in pluralist democracies than in state socialism.

A: You are alert, I see. But you have missed certain things. First, let us recognize that there are two problems of control that natural persons have in a pluralist democracy. One is the problem of controlling the state, and for this the natural persons can use intermediate corporate actors. The other is the problem of controlling the intermediate corporate actors. And you are correct, I described these—at least the large ones, which can be effective in controlling state power — as having an internally hierarchical structure, like that of state socialism. You forget, however, one point—and I will excuse you, for I did not discuss it—which is the fact that natural persons can control these intermediate corporate actors not only by voice, but by exit. They may withdraw their rights and resources from a corporate actor with whose actions they disagree and vest them in another whose actions they find more to their liking. I suggest you read *Exit, Voice, and Loyalty*, by A. O. Hirshman (1971), whose acumen in these matters will make up for my omission.

Q: So there is the possibility of exit. But in your argument there remains another inconsistency, for you describe how natural persons use the pluralist state to control, and thus subordinate, the intermediate corporate actors. Does this not result in a state indistinguishable from state socialism — perhaps we may call it state capitalism?

A: You have captured my argument correctly, but there is no inconsistency. The process does exist. If intermediate corporate actors come to be more and more under the direct control of the state apparatus—for example, if the university comes to have a large fraction of its budget paid for by the state—then they cannot act independently. But the existence of this process, this tendency, does not imply that it has taken the pluralist state all the way to a hierarchical state. It is a process to be guarded against, and I referred briefly to devices which do not have this defect that natural persons could use to control intermediate corporate actors. And if you are patient, you will see that in the next chapter, I discuss such devices at greater length.

Q: But I will discuss one of them now, since you already referred to it. You contrasted the German co-determination law, which you described as changing the rules governing relations with the law which created OSHA, which you described as a protective-agency law. Yet it is not accidental that one was passed in Germany, and the other in the United States. In Germany, workers have more power, so they can better use the state to protect their rights.

A: No legislation is accidental. But the issue is not what law reflects greater power of workers. It is, rather, what kind of device is used to protect natural persons' rights from corporate actors, and the by-product of that device in increasing the power of the state. For example, I could have used the Wagner Act instead of the German co-determination law. The Wagner Act, which changed the rules of the game between employees and employers in collective bargaining had a great effect. And it did so without greatly increasing the power of the state.

Q: To return to the co-determination law in Germany, you cite it as an important and effective alternative to protective-agency legislation like that which created OSHA. But is it effective?

A: In the Ruhr valley a co-determination law has been in operation for some time, since the period of occupation by the British. If that had not been effective, workers would not have supported a Germany-wide law. But the Germany-wide co-determination law came into being only a few years ago, and I know of no research on its effectiveness.

Q: I will press the matter further. You use OSHA as an example of an agency which need not have come into being but could have been substituted for by a rule-changing law providing for workers' councils to deal with safety. But what about other agencies, such as EPA and EEOC? What is the parallel to the workers' council?

A: You do have a point. EEOC is an agency which is set up to implement egalitarian social goals, OSHA, to protect health of employees. It is much easier to establish a law which changes the rules of the game for an OSHA-type goal than it is for one like that of EEOC, because EEOC has to deal not just with current employees but with prospective employees. They are not organized and cannot represent their own interests effectively. It can be put this way. When there are actors (such as employees in a firm) who can, if they have appropriate rights, represent their own interests or have some corporate actor represent their interests, then the proper role of the state, as I see it, is to facilitate that. When that's not easy to do, as is true in the case of environmental legislation or equal opportunity in hiring, the problem is more complex. A simple change in the rules of the game is not likely to be effective.

Q: Let me change the subject. Using your scheme, and returning to the example of the American Electric Company, it appears to me that American Electric is the agent of the directors.

A: That was certainly not Hacker's point. His point was quite the reverse. The directors were the agents of the American Electric Company. There is as a consequence a peculiar anomaly, an entity in whose interest actions are taken, but no one can say who that entity is. In the principal-agent relation, the agent takes an action (for which it is ordinarily paid) to benefit the principal, using its skills to do so. It was the directors who took an action to benefit American Electric, not the reverse. The directors were not profiting, they were simply carrying out straightforward action. They were agents of the American Electric Company. The question Hacker is raising is: is it not the case that in our society we have actors in whose interests actions are being taken, without our being able to say what or whose interests those are? This is both a conceptual problem and a practical problem.

Q: I want to return to the relation between intermediate corporate actors and the state. I fail to see the clear-cut differences between what you describe as the structures of state socialism — diagram (c) in your chart — and what you describe as pluralist democracy. First of all, these are oversimplified structures, and second, in pluralist democracies, I see many actions taken that are for the benefit of corporations — corporate actors, to use your term.

A: To be sure, there are numerous varieties of structural configurations in any real state, but if one abstracts the central tendencies in certain state structures, diagrams (c) and (d) reflect two ideal-typical modern states. I did point out that there are processes through which any real state moves in the direction of (d) or (c). For example, to elaborate the movement from (c), state socialism, toward (d), pluralist democracy: the subordinate intermediate corporate actors, whether industrial enterprises, trade unions, or local party councils, come to have interests of their own. Their usage of the rights which are delegated to them from the state comes under certain conditions to give them power which they are able to exercise on their own, making them less subordinate to the state. The result is that one can expect a movement of state socialism in that direction. The case of Solidarity in Poland is not a good example of this, because Solidarity came into being as an independent entity. But even existing corporate actors do come to have interests of their own, and sometimes they can reduce the strength of this descending arrow.

Q: You mention that Solidarity in Poland is not a good example of the processes you describe, and I agree. How then would you account for its emergence?

A: Again, I must commend you in your alertness. But again you have missed certain things. What happened in the case of Solidarity? First of all, the most important point is that there was one independent corporate actor in Poland, the church. There was a church militia whose first organized action was the keeping of order in the crowds during the pope's visit. This independent militia, unheard of under state socialism, provided an example of organized power independently of the state. Second, the leaders of Solidarity are practicing Catholics. In several ways the existence of this independent corporate actor in the state played an important role, even though it maintained an official distance from Solidarity. At the same time, the workers had received resources from the state which helped them confront the state. There are two important resources they did receive. One is education. The state finds it necessary, as all modern states do, to provide their citizens with reasonably high levels of education, to aid productivity. And it is argued by intellectuals in Poland that one of the major differences between young workers and old workers is the level of education of the young workers. Second, the state inadvertently supplied these workers with another resource, organizational potential. Grouped together within the same work places were age-homogeneous workers, between their late twenties and late thirties. That is a very age-homogeneous and active group, with a high potential for organization. The fact that age-homogeneous workers who had similar life chances were grouped together in the same plants and the fact that the state had provided them with education brought together two resources which led them to be able, together with the resources they got from the Catholic church, to oppose the state.

Q: You have not mentioned the use of the courts but only legislation. Yet courts seem important in the continuing struggle between persons and corporate actors.

A: Courts have been one of the principal instruments that persons have used, especially in the past ten years, to realize their interests vis-à-vis corporate actors. However, that raises a whole pandora's box of different problems, some of which we will come to in later chapters. So I will wait until then to comment on the role of the courts.

✧ 3 ✧

Risk and Responsibility

IN THE PRECEDING CHAPTER I examined something about how corporate actors come to gain their rights from natural persons, to have life breathed into them. In the present chapter I want to examine certain actions taken by corporate actors that have serious consequences for natural persons and how reallocation of rights can be—and in some way has been—used to restrain those actions. Then I want to explore some structural changes within corporate actors that will make them more likely to take into account consequences for persons in their actions.

One type of "serious consequence" of an action by a corporate actor can be described as *risk*. Certain actions by corporate actors impose risks on persons, increasing their chances of experiencing injury, sickness, or even death. These risk-generating actions have increased the focus of attention on actions of corporate actors, as exemplified by the following case.

A number of years ago, a company named Hooker Chemical Company dumped chemical wastes in a never-completed canal constructed by William T. Love. Only recently, these wastes have been discovered to have toxic effects on the inhabitants of the Love Canal area. A book was recently published, written by the man whose journalistic accounts exposed the Love Canal affair (Brown, 1980). The book's publication led to an interesting review by Eliot Fremont-Smith, "Love Canal ... Just a Tragic Occident," in *The Village Voice*, June 2, 1980, in which Fremont-Smith said in part:

For myself, the passion should be expressed in terms of prosecution for negligent homicide—that is, the forced personalization
of companies. Hooker is fighting the notion that it is in any way
accountable for Love Canal (the government, at last, disagrees,
and is suing in a civil action for hundreds of millions of dollars).
But I suspect nothing much will ever change, and no justice will
be done for society (no justice will ever be done for the specific
victims) without the repersonalization of polluting corporations.

The Hooker company may or may not have to be driven out
of business, but the people who ran and run Hooker, who know
what they've committed, should be put in jeopardy of jail. Were
I a prosecutor, I'd begin at the top, because it's at the top where
knowledge is most accessible and where the buck stops.

Which is to hint that nothing, no outrage, occurs in the
human scheme of things without specific people being responsible. ... As long as the companies involved are treated as mystical
entities in which no specific *persons* are responsible for anything
that goes wrong, there will be no change and no redress.

The victims have to suffer; there is no adequate compensation the country can afford. But some satisfaction shouldn't be
beyond our means. Companies should be prosecuted and heavily fined; owners and directors should, if convicted, go to prison
for what they are — negligent homicidal crooks who have, by
careful decision or willed ignorance, demonstrated their danger
to society, their need for rehabilitation. I used to think deter-
rence meant little; now I think it means a lot—and on the matter
of corporate chemical poisoning, I have no other solution that I
think might save our children. If ... the officers in charge of
Hooker several years ago went to prison, it would in one sense
be unfair—they didn't *themselves* dump toxics in Love Canal—
but I'd let them explain all that to Mrs. Whatshername, whose
chromosomes are crazy. [P. 35]

Eliot Fremont-Smith expresses well the outrage which
many persons feel at having risks imposed on them by impersonal corporations whose actions have potentially dangerous
consequences for them but which they cannot affect. One
need not agree with all that he proposes to recognize that a
problem exists — and that it is the problem created by an
asymmetric society, in which some actors, like you and me, are
small, while some actors — corporate actors — are very large,

so that an action they take may have consequences for many of the small actors.

One could express the motive which leads these large actors, like Hooker Chemical Company, to take actions with little regard for their consequences for small actors, like you and me, as the "pecuniary incentive." They take that action because it is the least costly. And in a competitive market, if they do not pursue the least costly alternative, they are driven out of business — or at least they fare less well in their pecuniary fortunes.

A second example, however, does not involve the pecuniary incentive. The example occurs in Cracow, Poland. For a long time after the recovery from World War II, there was extensive debate in Poland among art historians, restoration specialists, and paint technicians about how the artistic designs which once graced the fronts of Cracow's historic buildings but have faded over time should be restored. A few years ago decisions were made, and the buildings have been repainted, restoring the beauty of old Cracow.

But near Cracow is an aluminum plant with little or no pollution-reduction equipment, which generates large amounts of air pollution in the form of acid wastes, some of which are toxic. Recently, two things have happened: first,the exteriors of historic buildings which have just been repainted have begun to decay — not merely to lose their newly repainted artistic designs but to lose the very surfaces on which those designs were painted. Second, the people of Cracow and surrounding areas began to experience increased levels of respiratory diseases and other sickness.

The result is that the mayor of the town ordered one of three sections of the aluminum plant closed, after consulting with the officials in the central government. Then a different official called the prime minister, and the prime minister ordered the plant reopened, a decision which the mayor had to accept or lose his position. So once again, the surfaces of the buildings and the lungs of the people of Cracow are being eroded by the toxic air from the aluminum plant.

Here, the "pecuniary incentive" is replaced by the "bureaucratic incentive." The risk to the people of Cracow continues because the bureaucratic structure of the state means that the subordinate cannot go against the orders of his superior. Or perhaps there are both incentives operating in both cases. Both Hooker Chemical Company and the Polish government want (if we can attribute wants to corporate actors) to remain solvent, to remain economically viable. They have the pecuniary incentive. The agents at various levels of the hierarchy of these two corporate actors have the bureaucratic incentive: they want to continue to occupy their positions in the bureaucracy, which requires obeying the directives of their superiors. Again the comparability of the structure of the modern corporation — a product of a capitalist economy—and the structure of the socialist state is apparent.

So perhaps one would conclude that what is necessary is some worldwide regulating body, which fixes the level of risk, or imposes costs on corporate actors—governments or private corporations—costs that counterbalance the market benefits which arise from imposing risks on natural persons like you and me. There are two major defects to this conclusion.

One defect is that the balance differs in different situations: when the alternative is starvation, or even a subsistence level of living, then a set of persons might well prefer to accept a higher level of environmental hazard if it can give them food, or money to buy food. When the alternative is to do without a new stereo set, or to forego a vacation in the Caribbean, one might not accept the same level of environmental hazard. The utility of an extra dollar is less when that dollar is used for entertainment than when that dollar is used to sustain life. A worldwide regulating body, if controlled by persons on the verge of starving, would establish a standard of too high a level of pollution to satisfy the owners of stereo sets. And a worldwide regulating body, if controlled by persons who own stereo sets—as is more likely—would commit some persons to continued starvation and prevent them from climbing out of their poverty. Indeed, it is sometimes argued that *within* a country, such as the United States, the imposition of national standards by a set of persons who can afford stereo sets and vacations in the Caribbean imposes costs which are especially felt by the lower classes.

The second defect is very different, and to illustrate it, I will use an example. There is a contraceptive, as reported in the *Washington Post*, February 27, 1980, called Depo Provera, which operates as follows: a woman has an injection of Depo Provera, and for period of time she is infertile. At the end of this period, if she wants to continue contraception, she has another injection. If you have not heard of Depo Provera, it is not surprising, because Depo Provera is banned in the United States. It is banned in the United States because the long-term health risks of Depo Provera are uncertain. There are, however, more than seventy countries in which Depo Provera is sold where it is not banned.

The existence of the ban in the United States, which has no population growth, and the lack of a ban in some other countries where population growth contributes to malnutrition and economic hardship, is consistent with the principle of differing balances in different situations, as expressed above. The possibility of health risks may outweigh the benefits where other contraceptives are widely known and widely available, and where there is no population growth. The benefits may outweigh the possibility of risk where there is poverty and high population growth.

But there is an additional consequence here. After some period of use, it will be known whether Depo Provera does in fact constitute a risk to the health of the user. If it does, then the benefits may still outweigh the risks in some locales, and it may continue to be used there. But if it does not, then it may come to be used more widely—that is, the world may come to have a superior contraceptive that poses negligible risk.

This illustrates the second defect to worldwide regulation: not merely that the balance of risks and benefits will differ in different locales, but that a worldwide ban because of uncertainty about risks would make impossible the experience that would reduce uncertainty, and thus deprive the world of a valuable product that would, in fact, reduce risks that arise as a consequence of high population growth.

Such a world regulatory agency for drugs or chemicals could also err in the other direction, perhaps with dire consequences. If Thalidomide had been approved by such a body, rather than by national bodies in a limited number of countries and had come into simultaneous use everywhere, the consequences would have been far worse than they were.

So far I have spoken about two kinds of risks in which the actions of corporate actors are somehow implicated: hazards to residents in an area in which chemical wastes have been dumped or exhausted into the air and hazards to women who use a means of contraception that may have long-term health hazards. These represent two different kinds of relations through which the actions of corporate actors may impose risks on natural persons. The Depo Provera example involves a customer relation between person and corporate actor, one in which the person assumes risks by using a product of the corporate actor. The Love Canal and Cracow examples involve what might be called a "neighbor" relation between person and corporate actor, where there is no intentional interaction between the two parties, but the person experiences risk as a consequence of proximity to the corporate actor. Returning to the logic of Figure 1.4 in Chapter 1, these are both actions of the asymmetric type 2b, actions of corporate actors toward persons. More generally, four kinds of type-2 relations between natural persons and corporate actors can be identified, involving four kinds of actions of corporate actors that impose risks on natural persons. These are listed below, and beside each an example of the type of risk, ordinarily expressed in terms of federal regulation designed to cope with it.

Relation of person to corporate actor	*Type of risk generated*
1. customer	FDA-type risk
2. employee	OSHA-type risk
3. neighbor	EPA-type risk
4. member, owner, citizen	Agent Orange-type risk

By FDA-type risks I mean all risk imposed by a corporate actor on its customers, like the possible risk of Depo Provera for women who use it. In the United States, some of these are regulated by the FDA, but others are regulated by various other agencies, and some, of course, are not regulated at all, since some risk is incurred in the use of most goods. Risks of this class include things like risks from food additives, risks from medical treatments (like Depo Provera) with possible negative side effects on health, risks from children's sleepwear treated with a carcinogenic fire retardant, risks from smoking. By OSHA-type risks, I mean occupational hazards, some of which are covered by OSHA regulations. They range from risks of injury from work place accidents to risks of long-term health effects, such as black lung disease from coal mining or cancer due to inhalation of asbestos fibers.

By EPA-type risks I mean risks incurred by persons who may not be customers or employees, or have any direct relation to a corporate actor as "neighbors," but who are nevertheless potentially affected by its activities: they live in the area of an electric generating plant, for example, or downstream from a plant which discharges industrial waste into a river, or they ingest residue from pesticides used in agriculture. These effects are generically termed "negative externalities" by economists, and their defining property is that they are effects on persons who are engaged in no explicit transaction with the party who produces the effects, persons whom we might generically term neighbors. Into this class fall most "environmental hazards" like air and water pollution, and hazards created by industrial wastes as at Love Canal or in Cracow.

By Agent Orange-type risks, I mean risks incurred by members or owners of a corporate actor due to actions of the corporate actor. A large number of these are risks imposed on citizens by actions of the state, such as the risks to U.S. Army veterans exposed to Agent Orange during their tours of duty. They include also risks imposed by cities or states on their citizens, for example, by operating a sewage system which contaminates the water supply, or by failing to maintain roads in a safe condition. And they include risks imposed on their members by trade unions and other associations—for example, a union to which its members have delegated the responsibility of assuring reasonably safe working conditions in its collective bargaining negotiations but which fails to do so.

These four classes of risk to persons in which corporate actors are implicated derive from the four principal kinds of relations that natural persons have to corporate actors: as customers, as employees or agents, as neighbors affected by the corporate action, and as members. Sometimes these relations shade over into each other, so that no hard and fast lines of demarcation are possible. But recognition of these kinds of relations is important for several reasons. First, persons are themselves differentially responsible for the generation of risk in these different cases: As neighbors, say as residents of Cracow or as residents of the place that was once a dump for Hooker Chemical and before that was a piece of the never-completed Love Canal, they have no responsibility at all. As employees or customers, they are what has been termed "co-generators" of risk in deliberations of a National Academy of Sciences Committee on Risk and Decision Making, for the risk occurs through their action as well as that of the corporate actor. Customers use, and sometimes misuse, the product; workers pay differential attention to safety measures — coal miners, for example, sometimes remove their masks down at the coal face. And in the fourth kind of relation, members or citizens or owners are ultimately responsible for the risks their corporate actor (the state or its agencies, or the union) imposes on them.

A second value of this classification is that protection against risks, or recourse against the corporate actor which generated the risk, is differentially difficult in the different classes of relations. Employees are ordinarily best able to protect their interests in a relation, for their concentration makes them able to organize for self-protection. Indeed, union organization is exactly that. Customers are ordinarily less well able to organize, and neighbors are usually least able to do so. In principle, members are best able to organize to constrain the corporate actor's action, for they often have nominal control over that action; but in some cases, they, like customers or neighbors, are dispersed and effectively unable to protect their interests.

A third reason for such a classification is perhaps the most interesting: it leads us to ask about other risks which are not covered by the classification, such as risks one imposes on oneself (as in mountain climbing, skiing) or risks that one person imposes on another (as the risks to health a smoker imposes on others in the vicinity). Whey did these risks not come to mind along with the others? The answer to that question leads directly back to the asymmetric society, and some curious social-psychological questions about the asymmetric society.

WHY DO WE WORRY, WHEN THINGS ARE BETTER THAN EVER?

Two facts taken in conjunction provide the basis for a social-psychological puzzle. The first fact is that there has arisen, in the last two decades, an extraordinary concern about risk. A National Academy of Sciences Committee on Risk and Decision Making was formed some time ago and recently completed a preliminary report on the topic. The French government has established a similar commission. The Russell Sage Foundation in New York has recently initiated work on the perception of risk. The National Science Foundation has a section on Technology Assessment and Risk Analysis. A new journal, titled "Risk Analysis" has just been initiated. In the last session of Congress, 177 bills were introduced which contained the word "risk" in their abstracts. Public opinion polls show that people believe that life has become riskier in recent years.

For example, in a recent poll of the U.S. adult population, 78 percent of those surveyed agreed that "people are subject to more risk today than they were 20 years ago" and only 6 percent thought there was less risk.

The second fact is that objectively, the risks of premature death have been steadily declining. Between 1900 and 1979, there was a 68 percent decrease in the age-adjusted death rate (U.S. Bureau of the Census, 1976, p. 59; U.S. Public Health Service, 1980, p. 23). Between 1950 and 1979, the age-adjusted death rate from cardiovascular disease has gone down from nearly 400 per 100,000 to about 250 per 100,000 (calculated from data in U.S. Public Health Service, 1979, p. 154). If lung cancer (most of which can be attributed to the voluntary act of smoking) is excluded, the age-adjusted death rate for cancer has been steadily declining (*CAA Cancer Journal for Clinicians*, 1980, p. 29). Motor vehicle deaths have declined between 1930 and 1980 from 16 per one million miles to less than 4 per one million miles (National Safety Council, 1979, pp. 40–41). From 1968 to 1978, fatal accidents in the workplace declined 22 pecent, and fatal accidents at home declined 25 percent (National Safety Council, 1979, p. 10).

What accounts for this curious discrepancy: people are freer than ever before of the risk of premature death, yet they feel that things have been getting less safe? The answer, I think, is that the nature of the risks to life has been changing over time. And this change results from the increasing asymmetry of relations in society. If we look again at Figure 1.4 in Chapter 1, we can see what has happened. In the risks of the examples that I described at the outset — Love Canal, the Cracow aluminum plant, and the contraceptive Depo Provera — the subject of an action is a corporate actor, the object of action a person. All the risks of the four classes that I described — risks imposed on customers, employees, neighbors, and members — are risks resulting from actions of type 2b, actions in which a corporate actor is the subject and a natural person the object of action. We may think of these as the "new risks" in society. They contrast to the "old risks," most of which are declining over time. The old risks are risks resulting from actions of type 1, in which one person's actions impose risks on another — individual violence of all sorts — or risks that come from "nature" — that is, uncontrolled disease and similar events that were seen to be out of anyone's power to do anything about.

Nearly all the recent regulatory actions of government — not only in the United States but in other western countries as well — are attempts to regulate actions of type 2b. And it is instructive that even in those cases in which there appear to have been recent increases in risks due to actions of type 1, there has not been the same kind of governmental reaction.

For example, in the case of robbery, rape, and other crimes against the person, government actions (as reflected by the probability of arrest, the probability of conviction if arrested, and the length of sentence if convicted) have been going in the other direction, toward a relaxation of constraints on the person responsible for the action. And one of the few cases in which there have been attempts to constrain actions in which persons imposed risks on themselves is also instructive: the ill-fated seatbelt interlock in the United States. The law, passed by Congress, to require fastening of seatbelts before the car could start went into effect with the 1974 model automobiles. The law required action by both manufacturers and drivers—that is, by corporate actors and persons. There was no trouble with the manufacturers, but when the time came for action by the drivers — fastening the seatbelts — there was massive resistance. Congress rescinded the seatbelt interlock law with great speed, and the experiment in attempting to regulate the actions of natural persons was at an end. The government moved, a little later, to do what it knew how to do well: to regulate the corporate actor's action. In this case it did so by requiring passive restraints (protection without any action required on the driver's part), which were scheduled to take effect in the early 1980s.

So there is not one puzzle but two: why do we feel matters are getting worse when they are getting better, and why do we collectively — that is, corporately — devote ourselves to regulating the actions of our corporate actors, but not the actions of ourselves? I think the answers in the two cases derive from the same change in society: the extraordinary increase since World War II in the size of corporate actors in modern society and in the increasing importance of their actions, actions of type 2b in Figure 1.4, in the everyday lives of natural persons. These have generated the "new risks" in society. Actions of large corporate actors have consequences for many persons, and it is these actions we have come to fear. The fears derive in part from the recognition that in this asymmetric relation, a natural person, as the weak party to the relation, has little control over the actions of the strong party, the corporate actor. And thus we pressure our legislators to use the power of that one large and most powerul corporate actor, the state, to bolster our own weak position vis-à-vis the corporate actors with which we daily interact. That the use of the state to regulate other corporate actors may not be the best way to control those corporate actors' actions is, from this point of view, irrelevant, for it is the most direct way.

The fears also derive, in some of the cases, from other sources. One is the recognition that an action by a corporate actor that affects many persons simultaneously — such as a meltdown of the core of a nuclear power plant—may not only affect persons; it may affect the very structure of society. Another may be fear of the unknown, of different kinds of risks than we have confronted before. The shock with which the Thalidomide case was met probably stemmed from its horrible novelty: the idea that a pregnant woman might, by ingesting pills, turn the arms and legs of her baby into a fish's flippers.

But an analysis of the situation, which gives us a slightly better understanding of why we act as we do, goes only a certain distance. It does not tell us how we may be made to feel better again, to be less obsessed by the fear of risk, nor does it tell us how to be objectively better off, to be less subject to risk, without sacrificing the benefits by which corporate actors seduce us into accepting the risks they impose. To do that, we may ask ourselves another question.

HOW CAN CORPORATE ACTORS BE MADE APPROPRIATELY RESPONSIBLE?

For one type of risk, this question may in principle be more easily answered than in the other types. This is the member- or Agent Orange-type risk, in which a corporate actor takes actions imposing risks on some or all of its members, which has a somewhat different character than the other types. In the other types of risks, neither those in effective control of the corporate actor's actions nor those who have constitutional control of its action are exposed to the risks that are generated. But in this type of risk, the members who have constitutional control are precisely those exposed to the risks. What this means is that the solution to the question of the appropriate degree of risk may be fundamentally simpler here. Here, the appropriate level of risk may be determined by a collective decision, since those who benefit from the corporate actor's risk-generating action are also those who are exposed to the risks generated by it.

An example of an action of this sort is fluoridation of the water system by a community. Whether or not there are objective risks, the principal argument by those opposed to fluoridation has been the dangers of the fluoride salt used for fluoridation; for taken in large quantities, it is poisonous. Another example is the decision of a country whether to test nuclear weapons: the citizens of a country deciding whether to test nuclear weapons are both the persons that the weapons are designed to protect and the persons who will experience any radioactive fallout from the testing. Still another example is the decision by a publicly owned utility (such as a utility owned by consumers) whether to build a nuclear generating plant.

To see how the collective decision may, in this type of risky action, take into account both the perceived costs and the perceived benefits of the action; it is useful to see how utility calculations may be carried out. For an individual subject both to the risk and the benefits, most risky actions can be characterized as having a small benefit which will be experienced with certainty or near certainty versus a large cost which has only a very small chance of being experienced.

Let p_1 be the (very small) probability that the danger represented by the risk will actually be experienced, p_2 be the probability (near 1.0) that the benefit from the action will be experienced, C be the absolute value (very large) of the negative utility from the risky consequence, and B be the (very small) positive utility of the benefit from the action. Then the choice can be described as one in which p_1C is balanced against p_2B. If p_1C is greater than p_2B, the action has a negative expected value and should not be taken; if p_1C is less than p_2B, the action has a positive expected value and should be taken.* And since p_2 is near 1.0, we can neglect it, and say that if p_1, the chance that the risky consequence will happen, is greater than the ratio B/C, the ratio of benefits to possible costs, then the action should not be taken.

Thus the critical comparison is p_1 versus B/C. This comparison is of particular relevance for an activity called "risk assessment," which has been developed for aiding such risk-generating decisions. Risk assessment is, in its simplest form, the assessment of the size of p_1; i.e., the chance of a core meltdown in a nuclear power plant or the chance of a liquefied natural gas tanker exploding in a harbor. The usual assumption is that a risk-assessment group carries out such an assessment and then a central decision maker carries out the comparison of p_1 versus B/C and makes the decision. But for member type risks, a quite different procedure is possible, and in fact sometimes occurs. This is each citizen carrying out — ordinarily implicitly — the comparison and then casting a vote for or against the risk-generating action on the basis of the balance of p_1 versus B/C. In actions where the costs, the benefits, and the risk are similar for all members of the corporate actor, such an alternative procedure is in principle appropriate. Different members may evaluate them differently; but the collective decision results in an action in which (if the risky action is taken) the corporate actor imposes on all a set of risks to the individual members that they have judged not to outweight the individual benefits they experience from the action.

This has occurred on a number of occasions at the city level. For example, fluoridation decisions in cities in the United States have often been made by the city government only to have a petition for a general referendum. This became so common that in at least one state, the state legislature passed a law requiring all fluoridation decisions to be made by general referendum. And in other actions involving risk a similar popular reaction to a risk-generating decision has

---

*Those familiar with these kinds of calculations will recognize that this assumes no risk-aversion or risk-preference. Including such an element would make the calculation a little more complex but no different in principle.

sometimes occurred, leading the centrally decided action to be revoked after popular protest.

It would be satisfying to be able to say that this procedure that, in principle, allows appropriate balancing of risks and benefits — because they are balanced within each person — does so not only in principle but in fact. However, this seems not to be the case: the social-psychological evidence is that people systematically overestimate very small probabilities, which in this case means overestimating the risk. Their responses are also very sensitive to the way a case is presented to them, so that reactions are not only biased against risky actions, but they are also very unstable, depending on details of presentation that do not affect the actual risk, the benefits, and the costs.

It may turn out that more extensive knowledge of these reactions will make possible design of a choice procedure in which risks are appropriately balanced against benefits by persons who experience both. If this does come to be possible, it facilitates the decision for Agent Orange-type (i.e., member-type) risks. But for other types of risk, the question remains. How can corporate actors be made appropriately responsible? A calculus of the sort described above is not applicable except in member-type risks, for risks are imposed on persons other than those who control the corporate actor. The question is not a simple one but is complex in the following way. If corporate actors are made sufficiently fearful of imposing risks on natural persons, they will cease to act altogether, and the benefits brought about by their actions — benefits responsible for our current standard of living and our social order — will be dissolved. For example, the outcomes of recent liability suits have led one manufacturer of protective helmets for football players to cease manufacturing them altogether, and a question exists whether *any* manufacturers will stay in the field because high awards in liability suits continue to be made despite helmets meeting government-established protective standards. Or the imposition of zero-risk standards, such as the water-quality standard legislated by Congress, could, with sufficiently accurate measuring instruments and exact enforcement of the law, end all industrial activity that discharges water, as well as all urban sewage disposal. Yet on the other hand, without some form of intervention, corporate actors may be sufficiently nonfearful of imposing risks on natural persons that a much higher level of risk is imposed than would be warranted by any balancing of benefits against the risk.

One way of approaching this question of appropriate responsibility on the part of corporate actors is to examine the whole set of instruments that persons have at their disposal for inducing responsibility on the part of corporate actors: legal liability, government standards coupled with regulatory enforcement, the creation of countervailing corporate actors, the use of economic incentives to reduce risk-generating actions, and others. A different way, however, is to attempt an analysis—first assessing why it is that risk-generating actions of corporate actors are more problematic than risk-generating actions of natural persons, and then examining what it is about the internal structure of corporate actors that creates the problems. I will proceed in this second way.

There are four elements that differentiate risk-inducing actions of corporate actors from those of persons. One is the fact that being larger and much more powerful, an action of a corporate actor will ordinarily have much more extensive consequences than an action of a person. Sometimes these consequences are especially severe because they affect many persons at once, as would a nuclear core meltdown or pesticide poisoning. Or if, on the other side, a corporation stops an activity because of too great attention to the reduction of risk, it may go out of business, eliminating extensive potential benefits, especially to employees, but also to customers. For example, air pollution standards have made some industrial plants uneconomic, putting people out of work. Or if the current attention to risk in nuclear plant construction and operation is inappropriately great, and if this makes nuclear power uneconomic, then the resulting increase in use of fossil fuels, particularly coal, may expose the planet to the risk of irreversible warming, due to an excess of CO_2 in the upper atmosphere. These more extensive consequences, whether they arise from actions that induce risk or from actions that guard against risk, make the question of appropriate responsibility a more important one than is the question of appropriate responsibility on the part of a natural person.

The second element that differentiates risk-inducing actions of corporate actors from those of natural persons is that although corporate actors are treated as unitary "persons" before the law, they are highly differentiated in structure, and decisions that affect the generation of risk are made by natural persons at particular points in this differentiated structure. There is no certainty that whatever the constraints imposed on or inducements made to the corporate actor, designed to bring about appropriate responsibility, they will be transmitted with the proper force to the point or points at which decisions are made. A form that this takes which is especially frequent is an action of a corporate actor (say a government agency) toward a person which is implemented by the lowest person in the hierarchy, a clerk or minor official who is in contact with the person. The clerk or minor official can see the anguish and pain this action causes, and the reasonableness of the person's arguments that it should not be taken. But the response to the person cannot take that into account. It is only, "I'm just carrying out my job," or "I'm only following orders," or "My hands are tied. The decision was made at a higher level," or "I'll transmit your complaint to my boss, but you shouldn't be hopeful that anything will come of it." This is not to say, of course, that the person is always right, and the corporate actor always wrong in such circumstances. It is to say, rather, that the structure of the interaction is much different than that in the classic type-1 interactions of which society was once composed, in which the consequences of a person's action toward another were easily and directly communicated back to the person.* Here the corporate "person"

---

*It is true that the consequences of the actions of a powerful person, such as a king whose orders were carried out by subordinates, were often not communicated back to that person, so that harm could be done by the subordinates who were "powerless to change the action," just as is true today. This structural fault was just as characteristic of the old corporate actors of the past as for the new ones that abound in the present. There were, however, far fewer corporate actors, relative to the population of natural persons, than there are today.

is a complex articulated structure of natural persons, and direct communication often does not occur. A natural person is also a complex articulated (physiological) structure, but that structure has evolved in such a way that the consequences of actions as experienced by the senses are rapidly transmitted back to the decision-making center. That evolution has not taken place to the same degree for the complex social organization.

The third element that differentiates risk-inducing actions of a corporate actor from those of a natural person is related to the second: given that the consequences of action or the constraints or inducements applied to a corporate actor are insufficiently well transmitted within the organizational structure, the constraints on corporate action wil be differentially effective, depending upon the points in the structure of the corporate actor to which they are applied. Yet the principles of legal liability as they affect corporations and the assumptions behind laws which impose standards or costs to constrain corporate action seldom recognize this. The result is that legal liability or regulatory laws do not always have the same deterrent effect that they have for natural persons.

Finally, the fourth element that differentiates risk-inducing actions of corporate actors from those of natural persons is that natural persons' self-interested actions are constrained in two ways: internally, through socialization that begins at a young age and throughout life leads us each to pay some attention to others' interests; and externally, through sanctions applied to control behavior. Only the latter form of constraint exists for the corporate actor.

I will turn to the third of these differentiating elements and then come back to the second. I want to ask where the liability for action lies and will attempt to answer this question by beginning with a number of examples.

First, consider the following legal case. A bakery truck was going down a narrow street in an English town. The driver of the truck, avoiding a car coming from the other direction, swerved, the truck jumped the curb and sideswiped the adjacent building, smashing the front of a news-and-candy store which occupied it.

Who should be liable to the owner of the sideswiped building in this case? In the precedent of common law, the bakery owner is liable, not the driver of the bakery truck. This comes under what is known as the law of agency, and in the law of agency, there is a principal and an agent. So long as the agent is acting under the authority of the principal, the principal, and not the agent, is held responsible for the agent's action which harms a third party. If the principal is a corporate actor, this leaves unanswered the question of whether liability is ever pinned to any natural person; but it does make clear that it is not the agent—i.e., the employee—who is held responsible. Note, however, one consequence of this ruling: it does not induce the agent to be careful. It remains up to the corporate actor to do that, and as the carelessness of employees in many firms can attest, many corporate actors are not well structured to do that.

Consider next a case which at first appears to contradict this. General Electric, Westinghouse, and other firms were charged with having engaged in illegal collusion on the prices of electric turbines. The companies were found guilty but not only the companies; executive officers as well were found guilty of criminal offenses for their actions. This example appears to contradict the first, for here it is the agents—the managers—and not just the principal, which is the company itself, that are held liable. The legal basis for such a finding is interesting; it is the legal unacceptability of the defense that corporate actions can be taken without their being communicated to the principal officers of the corporation. Thus in certain cases high-level managers are regarded, along with the corporation itself, as principals of the action, and liability reverts not only to the corporation as principal but to executive officers as well.

But why were the owners—that is, the stockholders—of General Electric and Westinghouse not held liable for this action? This answer is clear: the principle of limited liability, which limits the liability of a stockholder of a corporation to the amount invested. The stockholder can only lose the investment and is protected both from civil suits and criminal charges resulting from the corporation's action. Here the law's assumption is opposite to that concerning executives in the GE-Westinghouse case: The stockholder is assumed by the law not to be cognizant of and in control of the action, though the chief executive is.

Now consider the Agent Orange case. Here the charge is against the U.S. government, against the state as a corporate actor. The persons put at risk are certain of its citizens who, as military servicemen, were exposed to a toxic chemical with long-term health effects. Who should be liable here? The state as a corporate actor? The U.S. president personally? If the latter, the president currently in office, or the one in office at the time of Agent Orange's use? The citizens of the U.S.? The Joint Chiefs of Staff of the Armed Forces? If there is legal liability in this case, it will be, of course, the state that is held liable, not the chiefs of staff or the president. But how is this different from the GE-Westinghouse case?

Consider next the Pinto case in which the Ford Motor Company was held liable for deaths resulting from failure to sufficiently well shield the occupants from the gasoline tank, leading to what the court held to be excessive risk in rear-end collisions. An important element in the case was that employees of Ford had considered additional shielding but had decided against it after a cost-benefit analysis had led to a decision not to introduce the additional shielding. One curious aspect of the case is the suspicion that the company would not have been held liable for the deaths if they had not considered the additional shielding and carried out the cost-benefit analysis. But the point of interest here is that neither the engineers who carried out the cost-benefit analysis, nor their immediate superiors who decided against the shielding, were held personally liable. This is consistent with the first case I presented, which followed the general common-law precedent: that the principal (in this case, Ford Motor Company) — and not the agent — is held liable for a failure to exercise reasonable care. Yet in contrast to the GE-Westinghouse case, no executives of Ford were held personally liable.

Now let us turn to a somewhat different case: the case of the Nuremberg trials of major war criminals following World

War II and the subsequent trials of persons lower in the hierarchy. If the principal-agent theory of English common law had been directly applied, then the Nazi German state as a whole, and possibly Hitler personally, would have been held responsible, but no one at lower levels in the governmental hierarchy. Yet many at various levels of the hierarchy were held personally responsible for crimes against humanity and sentenced to imprisonment for their actions. In this case, a somewhat different legal principle was employed. The protection provided by a bureaucracy to persons occupying positions within it was stripped away. It was not a sufficient defense to state that one was merely following orders. This was regarded as a mitigating circumstance but responsibility remained. This can be seen, perhaps, as an extension of the principle applied in a murder case in which a "hit man" is hired to carry out a murder: both the principal and the agent, the person who hires the hit man and the hit man who carries out the murder, are held liable. In the case where there are intermediate levels between the authority and the person who finally carries out the criminal act (as, for example, in the Mafia), then insofar as a person at an intermediate level in the organization can be shown to have been a part of the sequence of action that led to the crime, that intermediary is held responsible. In this case, as in the case of the Nuremberg trials, the person who carries out the action is held responsible for the action. The general thesis in the hit-man case is straightforward: agents are not held responsible for actions that, if taken under one's own authority, are not criminal, but they *are* held personally responsible for actions that are criminal acts as defined by the law of the land. The protective umbrella of hierarchical authority is in this case ripped away. The Nuremberg trials, however, could not use this principle, for these subordinates were not committing actions defined as crime by the law of the land. A "higher law" was invoked in these cases, with the actions defined as "crimes against humanity."

But one may ask in this case as in some of the others I have presented: why should the particular party have been held responsible? Why the *agent* in this case? Why not the

principal, which was the German people as a whole? One answer, of course, is the question of practicality: it is practical to hold a person or a small set of persons criminally liable, for they can be incarcerated. It is less practical to hold a whole nation criminally liable in any operational sense. But quite apart from practicality, there are other issues. In what sense was the ordinary German citizen responsible? Could a person be reasonably expected to be knowledgeable of these actions? Was an ordinary citizen in a position to prevent them, if knowledgeable? Was a lower-level officer in the SS who *was* held responsible in a position to prevent them? These are questions that were not wholly satisfactorily resolved in the Nuremberg trials, and they are questions whose lack of resolution has troubling implications for the everyday behavior of citizens with respect to their government in every society, but especially in democracies.

There are social-psychological aspects of interest in the Nazi war criminals case. One is illustrated by a set of experiments carried out some years ago by Stanley Milgram (1974). Milgram had a confederate behind an opaque glass sitting in a chair supposedly receiving shocks from a naive subject who was administering the "shocks" under orders from Milgram, the experimenter. What was most remarkable about these experiments was the amount of pain that subjects acting under the authority of a superior were willing to inflict on another person. Milgram's subjects apparently in some fashion were able to transfer psychological responsibility for their actions to the person who was giving them the order. As in the case of Nazis who operated the concentration camps with their gas chambers. Milgram's subordinates withheld the critical capacity that would ordinarily have monitored their actions and inhibited those actions which they were not willing to take responsibility for.

I have presented a panoply of illustrations of liability, or responsibility in civil and criminal cases, with different parties being held liable in different cases. Corporate actors ordinarily have members or owners or citizens, a board of directors or a legislative body representing them, a chief executive officer, and employees. There are cases of *each* of these parties being held personally liable as well as cases in which only the corporate actor itself was held liable, and none of the natural persons involved with it had any personal liability for its actions. What seem to be the principles adhered to by the courts in these cases? There is hardly perfect consistency, as there often is not in legal precedents, but there are certain elements that appear to play an important part. Ordinarily when the matter is merely a civil action, and no laws have been violated, no natural person is held liable but only the corporate actor as the principal in the case. The central question appears to be the exercise of reasonable care against negligence; but the limits of responsiblity to which a corporate actor is held in its product, its work place, and its wastes appear to expand as the asymmetry of the relation between corporate actor and natural person increases.

The case of interest, so far as personal liability within the corporate actor is concerned, is that of a criminal rather than a civil case. And that case is of interest because it provides a basis for looking more deeply at the internal structure of corporate actors. When a corporation commits a crime what persons are liable? Any and all? Or none? The elements that appear to play an important part appear to be three: to what degree was the person responsible for initiating or implementing the action? And for those persons who were not in this way directly involved in the action, two other questions: could someone in this person's position be reasonably expected to know that such an action was taking place? And could someone in this person's position be reasonably expected, if knowing of the action, to take effective action to prevent it?

These questions, and the fact that they are answered differently in different cases, suggest possible avenues to reduce the asymmetry of which modern society is composed. In some legal cases chief executive officers are held personally liable; in some cases employees at various levels and in various capacities; and in some cases even owners, who are ordinarily protected from liability, are held personally liable.

THE LOSS OF LIMITED LIABILITY
FOR AGENTS

A principle of the English common law has always been, as indicated in some of the preceding examples, that the principal, not the agent, is liable for actions taken by the agent in the course of the agent's employ, so long as those actions do not violate laws of the state. The principle in effect limits liability of agents—i.e., employees—for the actions of corporate actors which employ them. Economic resources of owners of corporate actors have been protected by limited liability laws since the early days of the modern corporation. In a very similar way the agents have been protected by the principle that they have given up control over their corporate-related actions to the corporate actor and no longer have responsibility for it.

This principle has always had the defect that it fails to encourage agents of the corporate actor to exercise appropriate attention to the consequences of corporate action for which they are partly or wholly responsible, unless those consequences are also made consequential for the agent. This defect is especially pronounced when the corporate action is the result of coordinated interdependent action of a number of agents.

The external legal changes in recent years designed to reduce the negative consequences imposed by corporate actors on natural persons have been of two sorts. One is changing the structure of rights under which corporate actors take action; for example, by changing the balance of rights in the relation between natural persons and corporate actors or by shifting some rights to the state. The other is by invading, so to speak, the interior of the corporate actor, to pin responsibility on particular natural persons within it.

This second direction of change in effect removes some of the limitations on liability of the corporate actor's agents — and by doing so, reinstates in the natural person attention to the consequences of corporate action for which not only the corporate actor but now the agent as well may be held liable. It is not clear just how far this direction of change can go, or exactly what paths it will take, but the general direction is clear. It is toward an "opening up" of the hierarchical corporate actor, seeing it less as a single monolithic "principal" or "actor," and more as an organization of partially autonomous components.

This approach is one pursued by Christopher Stone (1975) after a review of a number of legal cases involving corporate actions that imposed serious risks or other disabilities on many persons. Stone argues for a restructuring of boards of directors (for example, elimination of inside directors, providing staff for directors, increasing the extent of directors' liability, and inclusion of "public directors," responsible to the general public rather than the stockholders). He also argues for the establishment, within the operating officers of the firm, of persons responsible to the public (presumably appointed by the court), after a firm had been held liable in a civil or criminal suit. For all firms, Stone proposes the requirement of meeting certain information handling standards (in effect extending to other areas of the firm's activities standards now in effect with respect to financial information), to insure that the principal officers of the firm were knowledgeable about its activities which were likely to have important consequences for customers, employees, or others. This would insure that they were in a position to be responsible for corporate action.

As it turns out, restructuring to create greater individual responsibility is also the direction that various internal innovations within corporate actors have begun to go. If the law, in the prosecution of criminal cases, can locate responsibility for action at particular points within a corporate actor by holding certain persons liable, then this suggests that in milder forms of transactions in which corporate actors are involved personal responsibility might also be reconstituted. That is, it could come to be the case that the client would no longer hear from the petty official, "I'm just carrying out my job," or "I'm just following orders." There are several developments in the internal structure of modern organizations that indicate that this may be more than a possibility. I will describe several to indicate the direction. What appears to be taking shape is a social invention, or a set of social inventions, no less revolutionary than the social invention of bureaucracy, which transformed the form of organization within society.*

These inventions constitute a different way to insure that the actions taken by corporate actors are appropriately attentive to their consequences for natural persons. They do so not through constraints from without but through restructuring from within, through creating a different kind of corporate actor.

HOW IS THE STRUCTURE OF RESPONSIBILITY WITHIN CORPORATE ACTORS CHANGING?

Max Weber conceptualized the organizational form known as bureaucracy and gave it a central place in his theory of social organization. Consequently, it is especially interesting to hear what Max Weber, in a contemplative mood, once wrote about bureaucracy and about the prospects for the future of society (Mayer, 1943):

> It is as if ... we were deliberately to become men who need "order" and nothing but order, who become nervous and cowardly if for one moment the order wavers, and helpless if they are torn away from their total incorporation in it. That the world should know no men but these: it is in such an evolution that we are already caught up, and the great question is there-

---

*Some mention should be made of recent discussions of "moral responsibility" of government officials for actions taken by the government. The matter is slightly different in the case of governmental action, because those actions, in the case of foreign policy, are often not covered by law, and thus the criterion of legality cannot be used to evaluate the action. Nevertheless, the question of agent (i.e., government official) responsibility is similar in the two cases. Unfortunately, most of the discussions of "moral responsibility" propose no operational consequences for the action, quite in contrast to the World War II war crimes trials, and thus remains academic. However, it is interesting to note that recent work has moved into the direction of attributing personal responsibility to the agent. See, for example, Thompson (1980).

fore not how we can promote and hasten it, but what we can oppose to this machinery in order to keep a portion of mankind free from this parcelling-out of the soul, from this supreme mastery of the bureaucratic way of life. [P. 97]

Weber's pessimism was, I think, justified if one views this social invention, bureaucracy, to be the last of its sort. But let me give a few examples which suggest that it is not.

In the very early days of the telephone, when one spoke to the operator, one often knew that operator personally, by name. This was especially so in towns like the one in the first episode in Chapter 1, where the woman who was the saleslady lent her earrings to the widow. But this period soon passed. The operator became an example of the low-level agent in a massive bureaucracy, whose response to a complaint was the typical bureaucratic one, "This is company policy; there's nothing I can do." And when one called a second time to raise the complaint again, or to discuss it further, there was a different operator at the other end. Or by chance it might be the same operator, but one would never know. If one asked the operator's name, to maintain continuity between discussions of the issue, the response was likely to be resistant and uncompliant; for in a bureaucracy only the office or position is important; the identity of the particular occupant is irrelevant.

The telephone company has not changed very much from this bureaucratic impersonality, but it has changed slightly. When one speaks to an operator, the operator often begins with a name: "This is Mrs. Smith. May I help you?" Or, "This is Mr. Johnson. May I help you?" What has happened? It sounds like a response to Eliot Fremont-Smith's call for a repersonalization of corporations. It is not a large move, but it is a move in the direction of making possible the fixing of personal responsibility within a corporation—and thus making the corporation itself act more responsibly. Now when I have a complaint to the business office of the telephone company, I can maintain continuity from one discussion to the next, by asking the second time for Mrs. Smith or Mr. Johnson. Or if Mrs. Smith or Mr. Johnson is uncivil to me, I can report this to a superior.

There are other similar examples. Some companies have introduced a practice of having inspectors' names on inspection slips which go with a product to the consumer—presumably to induce a higher level of responsibility on the part of the inspector, but also giving the customer that identity, so that when an item is flawed, the company can assign internal responsibility to the inspector who passed it. These are only two examples of a variety of moves within corporate actors to link the person to the action, reintroducing personal responsibility for each act which, taken together, constitute corporate action. Neither of these structural changes will have much effect on the risks that corporate actors impose on natural persons. But both point in the direction of a kind of change that can translate responsibility of the corporate actor to responsibility of persons occupying positions within it.

Personal responsibility is not, however, the sole element of change. As the common law has wisely held, responsibility should be located where authority is. And to find structural changes which are relevant to this, I will turn to a very specific question: Why do Hondas have fewer defects of assembly, fits, and finish than do Volvos?

Honda and Volvo both introduced organizational innovations in their assembly lines. Volvo introduced "work restructuring," following the general theory that the single simple repetitive task of the worker on the assembly line gave no sense of accomplishment, no sense of responsibility for a completed product, no intrinsic job satisfaction. It restructured the line so that one person would carry out the whole assembly of an engine, or a small group working as a team would assemble a car body, which was "their" body for which they could feel responsible. Volvo's work restructuring may not have been unsuccessful, but it was not especially successful, in terms either of quality or quantity of output.

Honda has a different practice on the assembly line, not work restructuring. There is an inspector at the *beginning* of that line, who is part of that line, and who has the authority to reject any inputs (parts, partially fabricated car bodies, seats, doors, instrument panels) which do not meet specifications. The output from this line go into another line as inputs, where there is another inspector belonging to that line. *That* inspector has the authority to reject any of these outputs (inputs to that line) which do not meet specifications. The bonuses paid to each member on each line depend on the quality and quantity of their output.

What has been done at Honda is to give authority to the line itself, authority to reject its inputs and, correspondingly, responsibility for its outputs. It has introduced a new mode of authority in the plant in which each succeeding operation, such as an assembly line involving ten to fifty people, has authority over the preceding operations. I call this innovation "backward policing" because authority over actions progresses backward from the end of the operations, where the final product is, reverberating back to earlier stages of production. The earlier stages are partially controlled not "from above" but from the end point. The final goal or product is what shapes the earlier activities.

This aspect of Honda's organizational structure has been responsible for a quality of assembly, paint, body fit, and finish which is as high as any in the industry. This innovation does not, of course, solve all organizational problems, such as matters of design and engineering. Yet, although its success is limited to certain kinds of activity, it is clear that the backward policing of Honda is not a classical bureaucratic form of authority. There has been a change in the very structure of authority and responsibility in the organization — and a change which appears to offer some potential for reducing the structural asymmetry of society.

Another innovation appears at first to be of a different sort. It is described by Alfred Chandler (1977) as the multidivisional corporation, and Chandler attributes to it the success and extraordinary growth of the largest corporations. The innovation is one introduced by, among others, Pierre du Pont and Alfred Sloan of General Motors beginning in the early 1920s.

Each car division becomes a profit center, with the authority to decide to buy a heater or another component from another General Motors division or from the outside, the authority to set specifications on the components it receives from other divisions, and in other ways introducing pseudo-market transactions between the divisions. Each division has some of the characteristics of an independent corporate actor, although it is not fully independent. But it has a large realm of authority and responsibility. Again, as in the case of Honda, what has been produced is something different from the classicial bureaucracy. There are aspects of a market, this time not at the assembly line level but at the divisional level.

An innovation which extends this further is described by Donald Schon (1971), with the 3M Company as the illustration. The 3M central management took the role of financier for semi-independent enterprises, which were "spin-offs" from existing activities. The central company would, in effect, set up in business a group with an idea, giving them initial capital and providing them with organizational resources, but giving them both authority and responsibility for success and failure. In a fundmertal sense the organizational relation between the entrepreneurial group and the parent company is not that of bureaucracy. Just what is it? We can't quite say; it is simply one of a variety of emergent organizational forms which lie somewhere between a bureaucratic hierarchy and an open market.

Still a different innovation is that of the "rack-jobber." When you or I go into a supermarket, and find we need a can opener, we go to find one hanging on a rack, take it down, and pay for it at the counter. But in many stores, I am not buying the can opener from the grocery store; I am buying it from a "rack-jobber." Periodically, the rack-jobber comes into the store, fills up the rack, and collects money for those items which have been replaced, minus a percentage for the store. In effect, the store serves only as a location for the rack-jobber's goods and receiver of the money due the rack-jobber. Now are the rack-jobber and the store part of a single bureaucratic authority structure? Clearly not — we could not say which was in authority over the other. So there is an organizational form different from a hierarchical bureaucracy, yet not fully a market.

Japanese industry regularly uses in manufacturing a form

which is similar to the rack-jobber in that employees of
suppliers or component manufacturers may be working in
the plant of the final product manufacturer. This form, which
occurred early in the industrial revolution in the U.S., appears to be possible in Japan because of a closer relation between firms and suppliers in Japan than in the West (see
Williamson, 1975; Clark, 1979).

The franchise is another peculiar form of organization
which constitutes, if not a completely new innovation,
nevertheless a form that is rapidly growing. McDonalds Restaurants, Holiday Inns, Hilton Hotels, and a variety of other
things we could think of as "organizations" are merely clusters
of franchises plus a central body (which ordinarily also operates some of the outlets directly, as part of the central organization of the classic variety). Neither is it an open market. It is
an organization of sorts. But because a high degree of authority and responsibility lie with the franchisee who owns and
operates a single neighborhood store, this form of organization has a high potential for reducing the asymmetries of
modern social structure. For it suggests that if a large amount
of authority and responsibility can exist at this one organizational level — the level of the franchise — similar innovations
can occur at other levels, giving an overall structure which is
responsible at the level of persons and yet has the efficiency of
the large corporate actor.

I have described a variety of organizational innovations.
All would be described by economists as the introduction of
aspects of a market structure into an organization which had
the form of bureaucratic hierarchy. From the point of view of
the biologist, they would be simply different evolutionary
forms of systems organization, far less varied than the multiplicity of biological forms. But from the point of view of the
sociologist, the organizational innovations would be described
somewhat differently. They are reorganizations that remove
the conflict between one's own personal interests and those
associated with the organizational position one occupies. The
organization is restructured so that fulfillment of the person's
own personal interests and those of the corporate actor no
longer conflict. They are not identical any more than those of

two traders in a market are; but they are complementary and mutually reinforcing, just as the fulfillment of one trader's interests is complementary to the fulfillment of the interests of the party with whom he makes an exchange.

None of these innovations does this in more than a very partial way. And, unfortunately, none is directly addressed to the question of risks imposed on natural persons by corporate actors. Nevertheless, they begin to make possible, through internal changes, permeability of the protective covering that the corporate actor provides to persons who make its decisions from positions within it. The fundamental change produced by this market-like structure within the corporate actor is to reduce the disparity between interests of the corporate actor and interests of those natural persons who occupy positions within it. This does not in itself reduce the interests of corporate actors in taking actions that impose risks on others; but what it does do is make it more likely that sanctions imposed on corporate actors will be felt not only by the corporate actor but also by those responsible for risk-generating decisions. In addition, it makes more likely that those responsible for risk-generating decisions will take into account the consequences of the decision at the time it is made. If the law is moving in the direction of removing some of the limitations on liability that agents of the corporate actor have always enjoyed, then these internal changes, and extensions of them, make that direction of change both more easily implemented and less necessary. It is, for example, more to the interest of an owner of a Holiday Inn franchise than to an employee-manager of a centrally owned hotel to insure that the facilities of his hotel do not impose risks of physical harm to its customers.

It remains to be seen how far, and in what direction, these changes that begin to open up corporate actors can go, and how they affect the corporate actor's actions toward other parties. It is not yet clear just what the inherent limits of such reorganization are. However, what is clear is that, to answer a question I asked in an earlier chapter, we are not in the final state. The "new corporate actor" which has emerged in the past couple of centuries and changed the structure of society is itself changing, and it is likely to be very different in the future—possibly in ways that will make the asymmetric society less asymmetric than we presently experience it.

But when these corporate actors have *offspring*, as does the 3M Company among others, the offspring are not natural persons. And that leads to the problem to be examined in the next chapter.

DIALOGUE 3

Q: Let us take as given that whatever the changes in overall levels of risk, technology is continually generating new and sometimes novel kinds of risks to health. What do you see as the proper role for government to play?

A: The answer to that requires again examining the asymmetry of modern society. There are natural persons, corporate actors, and the one special corporate actor, the state. The relations of type 2 (to refer again to Figure 1.4 in Chapter 1) between natural persons and corporate actors have increased greatly in number and in asymmetry as the corporate actors have grown in number and size. The result is a large number of "new risks." In general, the actions of the government, as a corporate actor, can attempt to mitigate risk either through direct regulatory actions (actions of type 3 in Figure 1.4) or through changing the rules governing the relations between corporate actors and those persons put at risk by their actions. Where the latter can be effective, it is, as I have suggested previously, preferable because it has fewer effects in increasing the power of the state. Where the former is necessary, a principle that is wise—and that has begun to come about in recent Environmental Protection Agency practices — is to use as fully as possible devices that induce the corporate actor to appropriately balance benefits against costs. EPA has begun to use three such devices in fixed-source emission standards: "bubbles," in which a firm can, in effect, place several of its pollution-emitting sources under a single "bubble," deciding within that bubble how much pollution to allow for each source; "offsets," in which the same bubble principle is applied between firms in a locality; and "emissions banks," which extend the offset principle by facilitating the interfirm negotiations. Even greater balancing of costs and benefits is possible under a broader principle of marketable emissions permits. (For further discussion of these practices and ideas, see Kneese and Schultze, 1975; Noll, 1976; and Teitenberg, 1980.)

Q: I am also interested in the innovations within organizations — or corporate actors, as you call them — which lead to appropriate levels of risk. You described some organizational innovations, but I see no way that any of those would have prevented a tragedy such as occurred at Love Canal.

A: If you look carefully, there is a common element to the recent changes in externally imposed liability and changes in internal structure of corporate actors. Both of these changes involve an opening up of the corporate actor. The examples I presented involving liability in cases involving risk begin to answer the question: how might one get inside a bureaucracy or a corporate actor in such a way as to insure that the actions that are taken are appropriate actions? And the structural innovations I discussed do the same thing. Neither has progressed very far, but both point in the same direction.

Through both these types of changes I believe the asymmetric society is evolving in ways that do two things: (1) lead decisions within a corporate actor to more fully reflect the costs that action imposes on others, and (2) make possible the assignment of some portion of liability to natural persons responsible for a corporate actor's actions. One might go further to say that the form of evolution of the asymmetric society will be changes in legal liability so that liability can be traced to natural persons occupying positions. The Love Canal case may, however, be different. It may be only with hindsight that we see that the waste-disposal methods of Hooker Chemical Company imposed risks. There will always be some actions which appear to impose few risks in light of knowledge at the time they are carried out but are later discovered to impose greater risks. Asbestos mining, which was long carried out in the absence of any knowledge of the lung-cancer risks it generated, is an example.

Q: Is it not the case that private firms are generating a hereditary aristocracy among natural persons? I am speaking of managers and officials of private firms who are protected by the firm from "commoners." If a person has a high post in such a firm, he has a safety net. And these persons can only fall a very small distance, when they are picked up or their children are picked up. Private schools serve this purpose, among other devices. Increasingly, the IQ test and the SAT tests are written to favor their children. The result is a kind of hereditary caste which increasingly isolates itself from commoners.

A: Your statement seems to me a mixture of sense and nonsense. First, the sense. In every society, those with power — i.e., those with control over large corporate actors — attempt to use that power to aid their children. Thus private schools in the United States have served this purpose for children of the economic elite and are currently serving it for children of the political elite in Washington. In the Soviet Union, special schools for children of high party officials are used for the same purpose.

Now, the nonsense. It is not true that a hereditary caste is coming into existence. There is in the United States, and probably elsewhere in the West as well, *less* continuity from fathers' occupational status, power, and income to sons' occupational status, power, and income than ever in the past. As sociologists put it, there is decreasing occupational inheritance, increasing occupational mobility.

Q: To return to the internal workings of a corporate actor. You indicated by use of some examples how responsibility may be located and identified. From these examples, I can see in every case there was a person in the corporate actor who could be identified with a particular act. This kind of a solution seems to me to imply a denial of the corporate entity as an actor and the reassertion of the natural person as being liable for the organization itself.

A: Your point is interesting, but you should recognize where it leads. In any organization of parts, such as the human body, each part has a given function. But we do not deny that it is useful to conceive of the person as a single goal-directed actor just because we can identify the hand as picking up an object or the brain as determining what object it will pick up or the central nervous system as directing the action. A corporate actor involves coordinated action in the same way. Even the so-called decision-making function involves coordinated action. Although for convenience one may speak of a particular official "making a decision," it seldom is so simple. John R. Commons' discussion of decision making by union officials—with one official indicating that he always consulted "the action," an amorphous set of active members—exemplifies this.

There are some systems, or organizations, that are made up of undifferentiated individuals, yet we can still say the organization acts as a single actor. Once I was sitting in the woods and I saw what one often sees, a swarm of gnats. That swarm would expand, contract, would dart this way, dart that way. It was acting as a single entity, but there were identifiable elements within it. This is, I believe, a higher form of organization than a hierarchical form. Perhaps I am wrong; perhaps the swarm is in fact organized so that they are responding to a single gnat in the set, but it is very unlikely that they are. Very likely, they are responding to their nearest neighbor. Yet it is useful, because that swarm is acting as a single goal-directed actor, to treat it as a single actor. In language we do so by giving it a name, "swarm," and using that name as the subject of action in sentences.

Q: International law contains some principles of personal liability for actions. Is it possible to gain ideas about how corporate actors may function better from examining international law?

A: There is some history to attempts to pin liability for war. In World War I, there was a lukewarm attempt to try the kaiser; that is, to establish some kind of international law to the effect that there was a violation of the peace and the kaiser was responsible. Then, after World War II, in the Nuremberg trials, there were three different principles under which the international tribunal acted. One was the notion of violation of the peace. That is, an aggressive war was itself taken to be a crime. The second is crimes against the common laws of war. These are the international laws of war, such as treatment of prisoners of war. The third category was called "crimes against humanity," which were crimes committed against the state's own citizens, its civilian population. In the second category were actions taken against populations in occupied countries, such as Gypsies or Jews in occupied countries. In the third category were actions taken against German nationals, such as Jews in Germany. The whole international legal status of the Nuremberg trials is, I think, best defined with regard to the second of these three categories, because there are certain recognized general principles of common international law that are ordinarily observed in war. Violation of these is regarded in many countries as a crime. But the first and third of the categories were somewhat more innovative, with less legal precedent and less wide acceptance.

Q: This raises an issue that you did not treat explicitly. You tended to use the courts, not as another example of an asymmetrical institution, but rather as a background against which these asymmetrical conflicts could be handled. Now, on both your account and from many other points of view, the capacity in some societies for an individual to take his own government to court—as in the case of Agent Orange, where it is not the Vietnamese taking us to the World Court, but our own citizens bringing suit against their own government— that's very puzzling in terms of legitimacy and power and the like, because there's no apparent superordinate organization to which these two conflicting parties can go. There is something paradoxical about it.

A: It is true that there is something paradoxical about the courts. Should the court be conceived of as a corporate actor? If so, what kind of corporate actor is it? I find that a very difficult question, and the only way I can answer it is by the following analogy. I have done some work in developing games of various sorts, and some games require a game master or an umpire who is outside the game. The umpire is there in a sense by fiat, and it always makes one uncomfortable that the game is not self-governing and does not somehow run itself without this umpire or game master. Yet some games do require one. That seems to me to be the closest analogy to the courts. And yet, since obviously the court really is within the system, it remains a paradox.

Q: If corporate actors were, following your suggestions, to have to take consequences analogous to those that natural persons take, this includes death. What about that?

A: So let us examine death of a private corporation. What it would mean is that investors would lose their investment and the employees would lose their jobs. Yet the losing of an investment or the losing of a job is probably not a sufficient consequence to deter certain actions—and corporate actions are, of course, taken through decisions made by these natural persons acting as agents for the corporate actor.

Q: On the one hand, you are examining the conflict between natural persons and a corporate entity like a corporation or a government and trying to limit the corporate entity. And on the other hand, you seem to be trying to come up with methods to use the natural person more effectively within the corporation, to make the natural person king, for lack of a better word.

A: Yes, king. The problem, of course, lies in the fact that in their *collective* activities, that is, their corporate activities, certain benefits do flow both from the state, because of the social order that the state maintains, and from economic corporations and associations such as trade unions. Nevertheless, the ultimate end is to assure that the interests of natural persons are not lost sight of, are not submerged, are not foregone, through this peculiar kind of social structure that has developed in modern society.

For example, if we have a corporation that is owned by another corporation that is owned by another corporation, and so on, in a kind of pyramidal structure, then it can very well be that the actions of this operating company at the bottom might be far removed from the interests of any natural person because of a set of transformations through which those interests go. A very market-oriented and free enterprise-oriented economist, Friedrich Hayek, argued that voting ownership in corporations ought to be restricted to natural persons and not be able to be held by other corporations. There are, I think, some things about the emerging social structure that do threaten the realization of natural persons' interests. I believe we can see this in a variety of circumstances, such as in some of the examples that I cited. They will be even more evident in the next chapter.

Q: Suppose a group of persons only act together toward a single goal in one respect. Is it a corporate actor?

A: Yes, certainly. For example, when the families which were involved in the Thalidomide case got together and acted unitarily, then for a limited period of time and for certain specific areas of action they were very definitely a corporate actor in the sense I am using the term. In the theoretical framework that I am attempting to establish, a corporate actor is any body beyond a single person that acts consistently and unitarily toward something that could be defined as a goal.

4

Raising Children
in the Asymmetric Society

THE THREE PRECEDING CHAPTERS focus on a new social structure which has come into being in the past two centuries, a
structure that has spread with particular rapidity in the past
few decades. This is a structure composed not only of ordinary persons like you and me but also of another form of
person as well, what the law calls a "fictional person," and
what I have called a corporate actor. The particular form of
corporate actor which has spread widely is one with an internal structure composed of positions rather than persons, a
structure in which persons are merely *occupants* of positions.
Thus if one looks at the matter optimistically, natural persons
are freer than ever before, free to choose their corporate
actors and their positions, and free to move in and out—or if
one is a pessimist, natural persons are fundamentally irrelevant, in a way they have never been in history, to the central
activities of society. There may, in fact, be room for pessimism
from another source. The offspring of this new form of corporate actor, composed of positions, is another corporate actor, not a natural person. Neither does it provide a setting
within which natural persons raise *their* offspring. Yet in the
old social structures, and even today in the new, the offspring
of natural persons — that is, children — have been born into
and raised within a different form of corporate actor, the
family.

The family is a corporate actor of the old form: it has an
internal structure composed of persons, not positions. The
continuity of the family depends on the continuity of mem-

119

bership of the particular persons who make it up. Thus immediately the question arises: are there incompatibilities between this survival from the old social structure and the new form of social organization within which it finds itself? And if there are, what are their consequences for its functioning and its future?

To begin to answer these questions, it is useful to examine the fundamental change in social structure since the Middle Ages. As I discussed in Chapter 2, if we examine the common law of the Middle Ages, we see that a relatively small number of people were regarded as "persons" before the law, capable of making contracts, of suing and being sued. In the legal perspective of thirteenth-century England, women, children, serfs, clerics and nuns, Jews, and others lacked these elementary civil rights.*

We might ask how it could be that so many were without recourse to the law; how a society could operate with only a minority of its persons legally recognized as persons. The answer is that society was hierarchically organized, and that the person at one level had legal responsibility for and authority over all those below him. The household, a productive unit including not only members related by blood but unrelated members as well, was the lowest point in this hierarchy, and the household head had legal responsibility for and authority over its members. In the late Middle Ages, the hierarchy above the household had come to have lesser strength, especially in England, so that by the thirteenth century a household head was no longer subject solely to his noble's court but had the right to be heard in the king's court. But all those within his household were still subject to him as their authority. Indeed, the Napoleonic Law of France codified this authority and responsibility until it was rescinded, and traces of it remain until today in France.

Authority in the Middle Ages was decentralized despite

*Altogether, probably less than one-eighth of the population had these rights, for about half the population was made up of children, half the adult population was women, and according to Pollock and Maitland, more than half were serfs, not free.

the hierarchy but decentralized in a different way than in modern pluralist society. The decentralization existed as a delegation of responsibility and authority. At each level certain kinds of authority were held, with the remainder being delegated down to the next level. For example, although the free householder with land had rights as a legally recognized person and could pass his land on to his eldest son, the noble within whose estate his land lay had the right to take a certain amount of those lands as they were transferred from father to son and had rights to collect fees or taxes for their use (see Maitland, 1904; Denman, 1958).

This form of decentralization existed in a society where the only recognized repository of resources, power, and authority was a person. Corporations, associations, partnerships, unions, even towns were not recognized as legal persons, for the social invention of conceiving of an association as a legal entity distinct from its members had not yet arrived.*

When that social invention occurred, and following it the notion of the state, the way was paved for a different form of decentralization than had previously existed. A pluralistic form of decentralization, in the presence of a state with minimal authority over its citizens (no longer subjects), became possible. Power came to be held by intermediate organizations, no longer by single persons in a hierarchical structure. Successively, subordinate persons came to gain full rights before the law: servants, slaves, women. Society became egalitarian to a degree that had never existed in the Middle Ages; but it also became a less personal society. As authority of one person over another lessened, personal interest lessened as well. It became a colder society as it became more egalitarian and as freedom increased.

The family is the last institution to continue to contain strong elements of the earlier form of social organization. Until recently, family law kept married women from full citizenship status, unable to make contracts on their own, and

---

*The church was an apparent exception; but in the church all authority was held by the pope, who was regarded as the earthly representative of divine power.

under the legal protection and authority of the husband. Slowly, family law has changed, recognizing the wife's rights, but it remains a legal entity different from any other in modern society, with traces of the old hierarchical social structure remaining within it.

These traces remain principally at one point, in the authority of the parent over the child and the responsibility of the parent for the child's actions. It is no accident that this is the last kernel of the old social structure to remain, the last element of legally sanctioned total authority in a pluralistic society. For as each of the other "subjects" was freed, each could come to exercise responsibility and authority over self, with the minimal state exercising only that authority necessary to maintain order. Thus as servants came out from under the authority of their masters, this authority was transferred largely to themselves, and in small part to the state. But if a similar emancipation of children from the authority of their parents were to occur, then neither the state nor the child would be in a position to take over the responsibility. As a result, the "emancipation of children" has proceeded much more slowly than any other emancipation.

Nevertheless, it does proceed. It proceeds in part because the family is a legal anachronism, difficult to sustain in the midst of other social organizations in which persons are transient and only the structure is permanent. The anachronistic character of the family as a legal entity is evident in the various proposals that have been made for fundamental changes in the marriage contract. Most such changes have been proposed in advocacy of women's rights, in an attempt to remove inequality from the marriage contract. (See Weitzman, 1974, for a discussion of the legal and sociological issues involved in such a change.) Yet the proposed changes have these characteristics that would make the family unit more like other organizations chartered in modern societies. In particular, the essential difference between the traditional marriage contract and the contracts that have been proposed is that the traditional marriage contract gives the parties (in recent forms, both man and woman; in earlier forms, the man only) encompassing rights vis-à-vis the other as a whole, while the newly proposed contracts limit those rights. In effect, the newly proposed contracts resemble more nearly the formation of a limited-liability corporation, the prototype of the modern corporate actor.

STRUCTURAL INCOMPATIBILITIES BETWEEN THE FAMILY AND MODERN SOCIETY

The family is the prototype of the corporate actor around which the old social structure was built. The family was, in fact, the basic building block of that social structure. Throughout history, it has been a communal unit with pooling of the product. The *extended* family has been characteristic of premodern societies, and in many of these societies the whole social structure was built outward from the extended family to the clan and beyond. Muslim law, for example, contains provision for no corporate actors beyond the extended family, and the structure of society in many Muslim countries *is* a structure built wholly of extended families.

The family is often seen, even in the most industrialized societies, as the basic unit of the social system, the foundation upon which the rest of social structure is built. Superficially, this would appear to be true. Nearly every person in every society is born into a family, and most persons in every society are part of a family for large portions of their lives.

But in the new social structure the larger society does not grow as an extension of the family. The larger institutions do not grow out of the family, as the household, the manor, and the estate did in the Middle Ages, nor as the clan does in some premodern societies today. There is, instead, a sharp discontinuity, with the larger social structure built on a wholly different foundation. In the old social structure a woman's work was contained within the family and consisted in large part of activities that strengthened and maintained the family structure; and a man's work was closely connected to the family, most often a family enterprise which employed other members of the family as well. The family was, except for a few

esoteric economic activities, the locus of production —
whether of food from the family farm, of trade from the
family store, or of goods from the household crafts. Young
men and young women not only started work through family
connections; the very social structure within which that work
was performed was family related: domestic activities within
the family for young women, and productive activities as part
of a family enterprise for young men. The farm was the prototype and the dominant example. As late as 100 years ago in
1880, half the labor force in the most advanced industrial
nation in the world, the United States, was farmers, and more
than half the population lived on farms.

The new corporate actor from which much of modern
social and economic structure is composed is founded on different assumptions than is the family. It is a structure of activities, not of persons, with positions or offices as nodes of the
structure. A person is born into a family; membership in it is
what some sociologists call *ascribed,* while membership in
modern corporate actors is, by this same terminology,
achieved, that is, a result of voluntary choice on the part of the
person or the corporate actor or both.

These fundamentally different assumptions of the two
types of corporate actors can be described by focusing on four
ways in which they differ which have special implications for
the young. I will refer to these under four headings: responsibility and dependency, the locus of activities, personality
types, and norms. I turn now to the first of these.

RESPONSIBILITY AND DEPENDENCY

A modern corporate actor, as a structure of activities rather
than persons, has authority over certain activities and responsibility for those activities. A family, in contrast, is structured
around authority over and responsibility for persons. In the
traditional family structure the head of the family had authority over all members of the family, and even today the family
has nearly complete authority over its junior members. That

authority over the person carries with it responsibility for the person. In most families there are some persons who are economically dependent, and those persons who are not take responsibility for — and are held responsible by law for — those who are dependent.

This structural difference, with responsibility and dependency built into the structure in the old form of corporate actor, exemplified by the family, and not in the new form of corporate actor, exemplified by the corporation, has extensive consequences. Perhaps the most important is that dependency must be dealt with through special measures in the new form of social structure. For dependency is an intrinsic component of life. A person can be fully independent some of the time, and partly independent all of the time, but cannot be fully independent all of the time. Because this is so, some institutions are necessary in every society to take responsibility for dependent persons — the old, the young, the sick, the infirm, and those otherwise unable to maintain themselves. In the old social structure, in which persons were elements and were at a fixed position in hierarchical structure of authority, responsibility was easily fixed. Authority over a person implied responsibility for that person's welfare. In social organization generally, authority over a domain carries with it responsibility for that domain. And when the domain of authority is the whole person, then the whole person becomes the responsibility as well. Today a child is subject to the authority of his parents and is their responsibility as well. But in earlier days this was true as well of indentured servants, nonkin members of an extended household, serfs, and slaves.

As the old social structure receded into history (most rapidly in the last half century), it left a vacuum of responsibility. For when authority was no longer over the person but only over those activities carried out in the time given to the corporate actor, responsibility contracted as well. When the individual left the hierarchy of the old structure and entered the market of the new one, he left the protection of the patron and found no other protection to fully replace it.

For healthy, adult, able-bodied males, old enough but not too old to work at a full-time job, this shift from hierarchy of the old structure to the market of the new one is beneficial, even invigorating. For those at the other end of the continuum of dependence — that is, the old, the young, the sick and the lame, and for women occupied with child rearing — the shift has different consequences. It leaves them unprotected, in need of protection.

If this shift is to continue to its ultimate point, then not only will the family dissolve, the very concept of "earnings" must vanish also. For the family has been, throughout history, the essential communal unit, the unit within which "income" from the outside was diffused from those who "earned" it to dependents. The family has not always cared well for its dependent members, but it is the only entity, in either its extended or contracted form, to have done so consistently and effectively. In its absence some other means of allocating the social product, a means which is not yet apparent, would be necessary.

Parenthetically, it is interesting to note that the United States, which never had a feudal system, seems to be closer to this extreme than either Europe or Japan, both societies which have the protectionist structure of feudalism in their past. In Europe, there are in general more protective or paternalistic services for the dependent provided by that one special corporate actor, the state; while in Japan, there are more protective services provided by business corporations, the central corporate actors of the economy.* A number of Europeans of my acquaintance who have spent some time in the United States have commented on this, usually to the effect that "the United States is the best place in the world to be if one has skills, is healthy, and of working age. But it's not the best place to grow up, nor to be old, nor to be sick."

Special institutions have come to be required to partially fill the vacuum of responsibility. Old-age and disability insur-

---

*This difference between Japan's pattern of corporate responsibility for persons and that in Europe raised interesting questions for research. How far back in history does this difference go? Does it extend back as far as differences in the structural forms which feudalism took in the two societies? Did it rise through the different ways in which the two societies emerged from feudalism?

ance is one device which has been introduced by most modern nations whose social structure has been largely converted to the new form of corporate actor. Schools, occupying an ever-increasing fraction of children's time, have been another. But these specially developed institutions can — just as all other institutions created by the fiat of legislatures—be ineffective, incomplete, or inappropriate, or all three. In particular, the vacuum of responsibility for children is only partly filled by schools; some of the functions of child rearing which are abandoned as men and women focus increasing fractions of their energies and attention on those activities they carry out in the new social structure are not taken on by any other part of the system. And it is these abandoned functions which erode the process of child rearing in the new social structure.

The system of life-cycle interdependence through which young were cared for by their parents, then cared for their own children as parents, and were in turn cared for by their children when they were aged is broken up when children no longer care for aged parents—as they do not in the presence of old-age insurance and pensions. This means that children are no longer, to parents, a private good to be enjoyed in one's old age. They are a public good, and as with every public good, the fundamental question arises, who will pay the cost of the public good? That is, who will take the responsibility for rearing children and for investing resources in them? The question must increasingly be answered, "no one," as parents see it less and less in their interest to make such investments, and there is no actor at a level below the state other than the family in whose interests such an investment lies.*

*Economists in the human capital tradition will argue that the evidence is otherwise: that parents invest increasingly in the quality of their children, having made a trade off of quantity for quality. But only the decrease in quantity is clear. The apparent increase in investment in quality (e.g., investing in more education) is an increase in absolute levels of investment, but may be a decrease in investment relative to consumption expenditures by parents themselves. And in recent years the fraction of costs of higher education borne by parents has decreased in the United States, not increased. The state, which continues to have an interest in the "quality" of the next generation, bears an increasing fraction of the costs. In some countries, even the interests of the state have become problematic, as large numbers of the most highly educated youth emigrate.

In another way as well children were as private good in the old social structure: they were useful to the household even as children. On the farm or in the shop or in the store, before the advent of "full-time jobs" in offices or factories by adults, children were used and useful in everyday productive activities. The boundary between use and exploitation is a fine one, and exploitation occurred as well. But as production moved out of the household, children were less useful, more a burden, and the birth rate went down. (The contrast between rural areas, with traditionally high birth rates, and urban areas, with low ones, shows this clearly.) It is perhaps a sad commentary on mankind that as the exploitability of children went down, so did the interest in having children. Exploitation comes to be replaced by indifference. Children come to be no longer useful, either while they are children or when they are adults and their parents are aged, so who will take the responsibility for bearing and raising them?

THE LOCUS OF ACTIVITIES

As the locus of productive activities moves out of the family and into the modern corporate actor — a process which has largely occurred over the span of a century, though most of it has occurred in the last half century — this has created social and psychological dislocations for some persons. When the family was the central unit of production, all members of the family were close to those productive activities. The social life of the household and the economic activities of production were not fully separable: there were "spill overs" between them. Some of these were spill-over benefits in that much of child rearing could take place in conjunction with and be combined with the productive activities in which the household was engaged. The mother could watch the baby while she was churning butter or tending the store, and the daughter learned to keep house and care for children by helping her mother. The son learned how to farm by graduating from odd jobs to more responsible ones, or learned a trade by doing small tasks around the shop. Some were negative spill overs: the daughter was sexually used by hired hands; the son was kept in menial tasks and prevented from extending his learning.* But whatever it was that happened to the son or daughter, good or bad, it happened at home, and it happened in conjunction with the economic activities of which society was composed.

The psychological malaise generated by this structure, whether on the part of adults or children, was a malaise of *intensity*, a malaise resulting from intense and sometimes perverse relations with a restricted set of persons. This was the sort of psychological malaise which Freud found and about which he wrote.

The growth of modern single-purposed corporate actors as the principal locus of economic activity broke up this structure of joint production — production of economic goods, household services, and child rearing — by taking the man's productive activity out of the home and into the office or factory. As the scope of this shift increased, covering an ever larger number of households, it began to carry with it other activities as well. Social life, which had been age heterogeneous and focused around the extended family and the neighborhood, become age homogeneous, focused around a set of associates from the work place. The cocktail party replaced the family gathering. The demand for baby-sitters increased as children were less often a part of social gatherings of adults. And the baby-sitters' pay came increasingly to be spent on new forms of youth-specific social activity, which began with movies and graduated to other activities of which the rock concert is the most extreme.

All of this was less true for families of men who worked in factories than for those who worked in offices, both because the pace of work meant that social ties could grow up less in some factory settings than in the office, and because blue

---

*Vivid pictures of this richness of household life, with its good and bad effects on those within it, can be found in many novels. I like especially the picture of an urban craftsman's household presented by Bernard Malamud in *The Assistant* (1957).

collar workers were more likely to live in the vicinity of their extended kin. But the technological changes which replaced urban neighborhoods with suburbs hastened the process even among blue collar workers. (See, for an example of how this occurred in England, Young and Willmott, 1957.)

This evacuation of social and psychic life from the family and neighborhood left certain persons especially vulnerable. Women who were not in the labor force had once been at the center of society's central activities; now they found themselves left behind, while those activities had moved behind the closed doors of the office or factory. They were left in a social backwater, with children as their principal social companions. The household, which was once a locus of intense relations, now became psychologically barren. The consequence for women was psychological deprivation, which leads, as survey research has found, to lower levels of happiness for women than for men (see Bradburn and Caplovitz, 1965), and at the extreme, leads to various forms of psychopathology.

In recent years this psychological deprivation has, I suspect, been a major factor leading to the massive influx of women into the labor force. The principal economic and social activities had left the household and had taken with them the psychic sustenance that such activities provide; and the sensible alternative for women was to follow those activities into the work place, to recapture the sustenance they provide —despite the fact that this meant reducing one's attention to children and to child rearing. With this move, the splitting up of the "jointness of production" that characterized the household of the past was completed. That splitting began with the shift of the man's economic activities into the new social structure, and this move of a major part of the woman's life into that same social structure completes the splitting apart. Thus the productive and child-rearing activities are located in different places, specialized by function. The problems that women experienced when they were left behind in the home have passed, except for those who remain confined and outside the labor force. The problems remain, however, for the one remaining set of family members whose principal locus of activities is the home—that is, children. I will return shortly to the consequences of this for children.

PERSONALITY TYPES

I turn now to the third way in which the new social structure differs from the old which has special implications for children. Persons in modern society have been shaped — or spoiled, depending upon one's values—by the new corporate actors, which have given them a freedom and mobility that persons never had before. As a consequence, they are not content to remain bound in the one confining corporate actor which has not yet liberated them. Persons once spent most of their existence in an hierarchical social structure that was an extension of the family and mirrored its structure. The stability and continuity of these social structures did not liberate persons' ambitions; both the external normative constraints and the deeply embedded forces of socialization led them to accept responsibility, to bear unpleasantness when they could in principle escape it, to do what they regarded as their "duty" toward others to whom they were related. That last word, "duty" is a term which has almost vanished from usage, for its only relevance in a social structure composed of new corporate actors is to the "duties of office," never to duties toward another person.

This personality change generated by the new social structure is, I would suggest, one source of the increase in divorce, family dissolution, what some have called the crisis of the family. The family is a last holdout from a social structure of a different kind. But it cannot remain a holdout if its members are so changed by the remainder of the social structure— so enticed by the irresponsibility, freedom, choice, that they find there — that they will not accept the burdens of social organization that were once general and are now largely confined to this one element of social organization which continues to make demands on them.

The current generation of young adults, products of the postwar baby boom, have sometimes been characterized as the "me generation," selfish and unwilling to make sacrifices for others. But if the analysis here is correct, this generation represents only another point on a monotonic curve of increasing individualism generated by the new social structure. The individualism is exacerbated by the new structure of influences on purchasing decisions: commercial advertisements. For there is an interaction between the content of commercial advertisements and the dominant interests of the persons to whom they are directed: to a considerable degree, these advertisements shape their content to appeal to those interests; but to some degree, the content of the advertisements shapes those interests.* And the interests that are most easily nurtured and strengthened by advertising are interests of self-indulgence. It is especially easy to convince a person to spend money on the self. Thus to the degree that this process is operative, the growth of consumption at the behest of commercial advertising—purely an outgrowth of the new form of corporate actor—strengthens not only individualism but attention to one's own interests and needs at the cost of attention to anyone else's.

It is hard to find good evidence for the personality changes toward individualism that I have just described. There is one interesting set of data, however, responses of Haverford College freshmen over the twenty years between 1948 and 1968 to the Minnesota Multiphasic Personality Inventory . Between 1948 and 1968, there was a steady increase from 23 percent to 50 percent of freshmen who said "yes" to "At parties I am more likely to sit by myself than to join in with the crowd," a decrease from 77 percent to 43 percent who said "yes" to "I am a good mixer," and a decrease from 63 percent to 45 percent who said "yes" to "If I were in trouble with several friends who were equally to blame, I would rather take the whole blame than to give them away" (Wynne, 1979, p. 3). In response to these items and others like them, the freshmen at this college showed a steady increase in individualism and a decreased interest in other persons.

Of course, it is true that Haverford College freshmen may

---

*This suggests a possible type of research which could examine changes over time in the degree of self-concern as over against concern for other persons to whom one has relations: content analysis of selected types of advertisements over time, to examine the degree to which these are appeals to a person to make a purchase to satisfy one's own taste versus appeals to make a purchase to satisfy interest or needs of another to whom one has a relation.

have been a sample from a different segment of the total population in 1948 than in 1968, and this may be responsible for the difference in responses over this twenty-year period. However, the burden of proof would seem to lie on those who would account for these differences in that way, in the absence of external evidence that the selection of Haverford's freshmen has changed in a way that is consistent with the shift in responses.

Another indicator goes a little farther than these verbal questionnaire responses. Long ago the French sociologist Emile Durkheim showed a strong relation between the psychological state of social isolation and suicide, a relation which has been confirmed many times since. Thus the suicide rate in a population is a good indicator of the social isolation of its members. And between 1950 and 1975, the annual suicide rate for young white males increased 271 percent, a stark indicator of the increase in individualism carried to the extreme of isolation and self-destruction (Wynne, 1979).

NORMS

A fourth change for children and youth brought about by the new social structure is in *social norms*. Social norms are the historical precursor of laws. They establish what one *ought* to do, what one *ought not* to do, and what is *permitted* but not required to do. Or to use terms that have proved useful to sociologists, they establish what actions are prescribed, pro-scribed, and permitted by the community in which the norm is held. And norms establish expectations about behavior in particular situations. Norms carry with them sanctions which may range from a disapproving glance to extreme physical punishment for committing a proscribed action, and from a smile of approval to a hero's welcome as reward for a pre-scribed action.

The substitution of formal laws for certain norms, as is characteristic of modern society, has not eliminated norms as a means of social control. For law covers only the most extreme transgressions, and there are many degrees to which expectations may be fulfilled which never touch the limits defined by law.

Norms are important instruments of socialization, as well as important instruments of external social control given socialization. Because they are important in socialization, the content of the norms that a child confronts in different settings is important. If that content is consistent, that is, the norms reinforce one another, then taken together they establish within the child a sense of what is "right" and what is "wrong." If that content is inconsistent, and the norms conflict with one another, the child has a less fully developed sense of what is right and what is wrong.

In this context a critical element in the socialization of the child is the consistency of the norms to which that child is exposed in various settings. And in turn this implies that the social structural inconsistency between the family and the other corporate actors that affect a child's environment is important. In the old social structure the larger corporate actor grew directly out of the nuclear family: the extended family, the neighborhood, the community.* And norms were established—as they still are, in a much weaker form—by each of these actors. The content of these norms is conservative in a classical sense of the term: they tend to conserve or preserve the existing social structure. Thus the norms established by the family will be designed to preserve and strengthen the family, and the norms established by the community will be designed to preserve and strengthen the community as it exists. This "self-preservation" of the family or community occurs through no mystical means; those who have some

---

*Ordinarily, in the conceptual scheme I am using, the extended family, the neighborhood, and the community are not corporate actors, for they do not take purposive action (i.e., consistent action that could be described as goal directed). However, each of these entities can be regarded as a corporate actor for a particular set of actions, that is, the establishment of norms. And in some premodern societies where specific actions are taken by the extended family, the clan, and the further extensions of the family, these entities may be regarded as full-fledged corporate actors.

amount of power in a community are most important for the establishment of norms, and they establish norms which will not disturb the structure within which they have power.

For example, in a traditional community, power over the socialization of girls beyond the confines of the family is largely in the hands of older married women. The norm of premarital chastity, which is one of the strongest in those communities in which older married women do have principal control of socialization of girls, is a norm which at a cost of pleasure to the girls strengthens the stability of the family, and thus the position of the older married women (whose position would be the most threatened by competition from young unmarried women). And for the same reason, the norm is strongest when the male is an already married man.*

Popular culture sometimes reflects the functioning of such norms, as well as other nuances related to their efffects. Some country music does this especially well, for country music often recalls the patterns of life in the old social structure.† One recent popular song, "The Harper Valley P.T.A.," shows well the functioning of community norms, as well as their social class implications. In this song, set in a rural town, a divorced mother of a junior high school girl is reprimanded

---

*This is not to say that such a norm does not benefit other parties as well. For example, the norm of premarital chastity benefits the girl herself in a social structure in which her principal bargaining power in the marriage market lies in such things as her physical beauty and sexual attractiveness. This bargaining power is reduced if she is willing to trade sexual favors for something less than marriage. In a social structure in which a woman can have status outside of marriage and in which her bargaining power in the marriage market itself depends on other things such as income potential, this norm is of less value to girls. And one would expect to see it observed less. Those conditions are of course now present, and the decline in the strength and observance of the norm of premarital chastity is very likely due to this change as well as to the reduction in strength of the community. See, for an earlier note on this in a period before the last decade and a half's decline of the norm of premarital chastity, Coleman (1966).

†It is possible, in fact, that the current and recent popularity of country music in the United States represents a kind of collective nostalgia in a population caught in the transition from the old to the new social structure and not comfortable with some aspects of the new.

by the local PTA (through a note sent home with her daughter) for what the PTA regards as her improper behavior. She thereupon goes to a PTA meeting and proceeds to indict each of the board members for behavior which, though hidden, is more immoral than the behavior she is accused of (which apparently consists largely of sexually enticing forms of dress, as well as the simple fact of her existence as an attractive divorcée in the community). The board members are all leading citizens of the community, while she is of marginal social status. The song, which has subsequently become the basis for a television show, captures not only the functioning of the norms in such a community, but the hypocrisy often necessary to the maintenance of such norms, and the functioning of such norms in maintaining both the social structure and the power of those persons in it who already have power.

The genesis of norms in a society with extensive mass media controlled by corporate actors of the new form is quite different. The norm generated is a by-product, sometimes even an accidental one, of the interests of the corporate actor in gaining an audience or in changing attitudes to favor its interests. Part of this occurs through advertising, part through movies, novels, and music. The extensive use of sex in both these areas exemplifies this well: the use of sex attracts attention, and attention is important both to advertisers and to purveyors of entertainment generally.

What this means in effect is that insofar as such advertisements or entertainment escapes those community norms which would suppress certain content, this content (such as that treating disapproved sexual activity favorably, or that treating use of alcohol or drugs or cigarettes — or any other activities or styles of behavior which community norms disapprove — favorably) begins to establish a new set of norms, which makes permissible or even brings prestige to actions which the old norms proscribed. Advertisements and entertainment escape those norms when they are no longer locally produced by persons or small corporate actors within the community but are produced in a distant urban setting (such as New York or Hollywood) by agents of corporate actors. These agents or employees are not only freed from local norms; they, just like the agents of a company which dumps chemical wastes without adequate safeguards, are not held personally responsible for their actions, which are merely part of "doing their job."

The result of this is that slowly, over time, as mass media carrying content created by these purposive corporate actors occupies an increasing part of persons' attention, the norms of society come to be shaped by these corporate actors — in some cases intentionally, as the interests of corporate actors like those which produce alcohol infiltrate the content of the media;* in some cases accidentally, as a byproduct of the corporate actor's pursuit of its purpose. One of the most pervasive changes is the replacement of frugality as an admirable personality trait by an admiration for high consumption. There are, of course, attempts to reimpose norms at a national level, but unlike other risks to which corporate actors expose persons, these are in considerable part protected by an overarching norm of freedom of speech. When the constraints imposed on such content shift from the informal sanctions imposed personally in a local community to formal legal constraints imposed on corporate actors at a national level, they are in all but the most extreme cases barred by the legal proscriptions against any constraints on freedom of speech.

Although this is not the point to examine the matter in detail, it is clear that just as in decisions of corporate actors about risks involving health, which I discussed in the preceding chapter, there are various ways, apart from government regulation, through which the interests of natural persons can come to play a greater part in corporate decisions, involving content of the mass media. And it is equally clear that there is much to be learned in this new structure of norm generation with which society is confronted. (I should say parenthetically that the disjuncture between the old and new structure in their generation of norms is far greater in many areas of the

*For example, agents of scotch or bourbon producers have been known to pay producers of movies to insure that a drink which is poured in a scene is identified as scotch (or bourbon).

third world than in the United States. In many third world countries, television has brought a sudden invasion of new content from Hollywood, California, U.S.A., which subverts a large number of both mild and strong normative proscriptions in those communities.)

The consequence of this changed structure and content of norms is greatest for children. The normative reinforcement which the community once provided for the parent has been replaced by content which is disconnected from and often subversive to parental prescriptions and proscriptions.

An interesting and suggestive indicator of the impact of this change on the orientations of persons in society is given by another item from the MMPI given to Haverford freshmen in 1948 through 1968. In 1948, 29 percent said "yes" to "When a man is with a woman he is usually thinking about things related to her sex." By 1968, there had been a fairly steady increase from 29 percent to 43 percent saying "yes" to this (Wynne, 1979).

CONSEQUENCES FOR CHILD REARING

It is unnecessary to discuss at length the further consequences of these four structural changes for children in the new social structure, for I have touched upon the consequences in what I have already said. It is useful, however, to mention two that are not self-evident. One is a consequence of the shift in locus of activities.

The shift in locus of activities means that the parents' productive work—indeed, major portions of their adult lives — are carried out in settings where there are no children. Most adults will find no children in their vicinity during the day, every day from Monday to Friday, for adults are embedded in their age-specific corporate actors, while children are embedded in theirs.

Although this has some ill consequences for adults, making them less tolerant of and understanding of children, it has even more serious consequences for children—for they fail to see adults in their daily productive activities, fail to gain a sense of what their parents — and other adults — do for a living, fail in a fundamental sense to become socialized to adulthood. A consequence of this is that they become less tolerant of and understanding of adults. A second consequence is that as they themselves grow into adulthood, they are not well prepared for adulthood, and have a more difficult time making the transition.

Another consequence of these changes can be seen in the current crisis of authority in the high schools in the United States. Schools have traditionally acted *in loco parentis*, exercising authority as delegated to them by parents. What has happened over the past twenty years has been an increase in what has been called "childrens' rights" in school. A principal way this has come about has been via court decisions. A parent would challenge the school's right to expel or otherwise discipline a child, whose civil rights were—it was argued—thereby violated. Slowly, the court, which had itself acted *in loco parentis,* deciding each case on the basis of what it regarded as best for the child, began to act from a new set of principles involving explicit civil rights of the child, including, for example, the right of due process before explusion from school. The school came to be in an untenable position because, disciplining a child under the principle of authority delegated to it by parents, it found its right to do so challenged by one of those same parents.

Parents have increasingly come to truncate the period of their authority over and responsibility for children. This occurred first at the college level, for colleges also acted *in loco parentis* until about the 1960s, when that principle no longer held at the college level. Parents began to relinquish the right to exercise authority—through the college authorities—over their unmarried dependent children's dress and living arrangements.

The truncation has now occurred for some parents at the high school level, and faced with the absence of parental consensus about the scope of the school's authority, the court and the school have no alternative but to abandon the principle, now become fiction, that they are acting under a grant of authority from a parental community with a set of norms expressing that community's consensus. Confronted with the child's right to twelve years of free schooling, many public school authorities have not found a new principle under which they can exercise sufficient authority to impose academic and disciplinary demands on students. A further consequence is a decline in cognitive achievement, which some observers attribute directly to an increase in parental negligence (Levine, 1980).*

And when we ask why some parents have come to truncate their period of authority over and responsibility for children, the answer appears to lie in the principles of the new social structure: there is no room in it for authority over and responsibility for whole persons, only for portions of their activities. The family is established under a different set of principles, but the family is in a hostile environment composed of the new corporate actors. And those new corporate actors have begun to change the personalities of natural persons, in ways I have described, so that their concerns and interests are increasingly individualistic. It takes no predictive genius to recognize that as the children of the generation now in its thirties comes to populate the high schools, the high schools will have even less a grant of parental authority than they now do, and will be successful only if they find a different basis of authority under which to function. For the parents, having pursued their adult leisure activities for some years in the new social structure of modern corporate actors before "beginning a family," will be eager to end their child-rearing obligations and return to the attractions of that new social structure.

This is a part of a structural change that has made child rearing itself a smaller component of an adult's life. The period of childbirth for many women once covered the ages from twenty to the late thirties, making the period of child

---

*Consistent with this hypothesis is the fact that the decline is concentrated in the high school years, and it is greatest among students from middle-class backgrounds, where the conditions for early truncation of responsibility and authority are most prevalent.

rearing from the arrival of the first child until the last one left home about thirty-five years. This period was the major portion of the adult's lifetime, making child rearing the central activity of adults. The length of the period also meant an overlap of generational families, as the child rearing of the oldest children began before the parental family had been broken up by the youngest leaving home.

Adults who begin a family in their late twenties or even thirties, and have one child or two closely spaced, experience a total child rearing period of less than twenty years. It begins late and ends early, and it no longer covers the major portion of adult life. The interests of adults in their family thus comes, purely as a consequence of this, to be a sharply reduced portion of their total set of interests as adults.

What I have tried to do in the points I have sketched is to give a sense of the scope of changes created for children and for the activity of raising children in the new social structure. This is, of course, only a sketch, and goes beyond what we know through systematic research. Certainly research could —and should—be done in examining more fully the nature of these changes and the extent of their consequences for children. Before we go very far toward prescribing possible ways to blunt the negative impacts of the new social structure and find ways to put that structure to positive use for the benefit of children, it is necessary to describe the changes themselves and their consequences more precisely.

But I do not want to leave you wholly without any indications of what structural changes might take place. I will do so by first coming back to what I called the "spill overs" to child rearing from other activities. A central question in deciding how child rearing is best accomplished in society is a question of spill overs: whether the net spill-over benefits from child rearing being carried out in the context of a rich set of other activities outweigh the other losses that occur in such a combined setting. These are losses in efficiency in the adult activities as well as contamination of the young by the rich set of other activities.

I believe the question has not ordinarily been put in this fashion and as a consequence has, as I have suggested, been prematurely answered by increasing specialization, which increasingly isolates the activities of the young from those of adults. The inefficiencies in other activities that result from mixing children and child care in with them are reflected rather directly and immediately in the market: adults are less productive with children around, and it pays the corporate actor which employs them to exclude children and use part of the surplus to hire a teacher to substitute for them. On the other side, however, the spill-over benefits that are lost by such segregation of activities are not directly reflected in the market and do not have their effects until sometime in the future (and the causal connection may be obsure as well). Thus they cannot act to balance out against the efficiencies of specialization through the "invisible hand" of the market, resulting in an optimum degree of specialization. This different relation to the market of the two directions of effects of specialization means that the "natural" market forces will lead to continuing specialization and segregation of child-rearing activities, whether or not it is best in the long run for the society.

AGE-BALANCED ORGANIZATIONS

There is a form of social organization that would move in precisely the opposite direction, toward a reintegration of these child-rearing activities with the ongoing productive activities of the society. This form is the "age-balance organization." The idea of the age-balanced organization derives from two premises. First, in some form, the modern, voluntaristic, purposive corporate actors will be the structural unit on which the society of the future will be based. Second, society's survival depends on raising new generations in close proximity with adults engaged in their functional adult roles in society. If either of these premises is incorrect, then such a radical solution is not necessary. But if they are correct, then some solution approximating this one is necessary to the survival of society.

In practice, the age-balanced organization would be a work organization, whether largely white collar or largely blue collar, with one difference: its age structure would approximately mirror the age structure of the society. This means that the organization would contain within it, during the working day, children from a very young age to older persons who do not hold a full-time job. The organization would necessarily contain a greater mix of activities than at present, because there would be explicit learning settings. The mix should extend down to the level of the individual person, with nearly all persons spending some time in productive settings, some time in learning settings, and some time in teaching settings; and it should extend even to the level of the activity itself, with many more activities than at present combining productivity and learning. The particular way a given organization would structure itself would be determined from within the organization; the principal external requirement would be that the organization take responsibility, during the working day, for a quota of young and old in the same proportion to those in between as found in society as a whole.

Obviously, such organizations could not operate within the private sector of the economy unless they received a public subsidy or reduced taxation equivalent to their public functions (since the organization would be carrying out functions ordinarily carried out by public institutions), and obviously, some kind of general inspection procedures would be necessary. Within the public sector, organizations such as government agencies could carry out such functions, the subsidy in that case being expressed simply as a larger budgetary allocation. Because of this the first experimentation with age-balanced organizations would most easily be carried out in public-sector organizations.

The description above may sound curious indeed, for we are accustomed to a very different organizaton of society. Yet if we reflect, we should recognize that never in history until the twentieth century have the young of society been largely separated from the ongoing productive activities of that society. The form of organization under which we currently live is a very new one, and as I have indicated in earlier sections, it has very strong consequences for the young, having greatly disrupted the principal child-rearing institution, the family.

As I suggested, I have outlined one possible structural change to overcome some of the problems for children created by the asymmetric society. I do so principally as a device to initiate the discussion of such changes — for unless we take some action to do so, we may become the first species to forget how to appropriately raise its young.

DIALOGUE 4

Q: How do you fit the problems and concerns you have described with the movement called the Moral Majority?

A: The existence of movements like the Moral Majority reflects a malaise which ordinarily is poorly understood but a malaise which focuses around exactly this change that I've described, the change from the old social structure to the new. It is easy to find simple solutions, and that is what organizations like the Moral Majority do with attempts to return to the past. The problems and the malaise are not solely created by government, nor solely created by corporations, but by both, by the corporate structure of society. One must distinguish between the malaise which leads people to feel that something is not right with society and the kind of solution which they often come to.

Q: How would you begin to reconcile the economies of scale that exist even in artistic efforts; for example, the need for quality cinema to distribute nationally with variations in community standards, those that vary, for example, from one locale to another?

A: That is a problem created by the change in technology which has accompanied this change in social structure. It is a problem which can be to some degree mitigated. For example, I think the decision of the Supreme Court to allow local communities to establish their own obscenity limits within the constitutional framework was a wise decision. I trust the inventiveness of entertainment-generating corporate actors to learn to cope with this. However, such a ruling does not go very far because, like most legal actions, obscenity laws can deal with only the most extreme cases, even at the local community level. Clearly we cannot go back to locally generated entertainment. But we're only in the infancy of the kinds of entertainment which is nationally generated, and as someone from the third world would see it when they're exposed to largely American television, internationally generated. I have no solutions for this; clearly we cannot go back to the past. What I have done is to outline some problems. I have presented one social structural change which addresses a fraction of these problems, but this is one of the problems that it does not touch.

Q: Some people suggest that the development of telecommunications, allowing people to work from their homes, together with the increasing cost of gasoline and transportation, might lead over the next couple of decades to a movement back into the homes for adults. If that were to happen, what do you think would be the effect?

A: That has been suggested, and it is an interesting development. Certainly it is now possible technologically for a large portion of many people's everyday work activities to be carried out at home. I once confronted a similar question with regard to mass media communication technology and the education of children. Would it not be the case, it was asked, that this would mean the demise of the school since the technology which exists can provide better instruction at a cheaper cost without children even coming to school? My answer was that while in principle this could occur, the social functions of the school, including the baby-sitting function, will mean that it will not happen in fact. One might say a similar thing with regard to the work place. The work place serves social functions for those in it — and, in fact, I believe this is a major reason why women have abandoned the home for the work place.

Q: You concluded with the statement that we might forget how to raise our own offspring. But why should we feel that the specialists in raising children, the specialists in preschool education and elementary education and secondary education, will not in fact know better how

*to raise children than we ever could back in the more communal sort
of society that we had before?*

A: They certainly may *know* better how to do so. However, that does not mean they *will* do better. Professor Urie Bronfenbrenner, who is one of the most astute students of child rearing, recently summarized the state of knowledge about the conditions necessary for the emotional development of children. He specified four propositions, and the first was this: "In order to develop normally, a child needs the enduring, irrational involvement of one or more adults in care and joint activity with the child" (Bronfenbrenner, 1980, p. 1). The specialists, unfortunately, do not have this enduring, irrational involvement.

Q: But I must persist. Perhaps the new institutions that develop will structure appropriately the relations between generations. As the school becomes the place where children are socialized and where they spend most of their time, the entire society becomes conscious of its support for the school system. And in recent years, for the first time we have begun to consider national policy for schools. At the same time, as the elderly can no longer rely on their children, if they ever could, Social Security and other forms of transfer payments become the mechanisms through which the elderly are cared for in this society. In fact, for some time we have been developing in this society ways of responding as a whole to the care of the young through the school system, and ways of responding to the needs of the elderly, and also to the disabled, through still another system of transfer payments.

A: It has yet to be shown that the assumption of dependency on a very large scale carries with it the humane quality that is necessary to fulfill the needs of that dependency. Many states in the U.S. have found that the assumption of responsibility by a large corporate actor, an agency of the state, rather than by natural persons or a corporate actor like the family which is an amalgam of natural persons, leads to people getting administratively lost. It leads to inhumane actions that occur accidentally because of inattention, because, as Bronfenbrenner would put it, of the lack of enduring irrational involvement of other persons. I am not arguing against the development of institutions; but I am arguing that we do not know much about how to construct appropriate institutions.

It may or may not be that "appropriate technology" in many places is small scale, but it is certainly the case that one requirement for an appropriate institution for the care of dependents *is* that it be small scale, and a corporate actor composed of persons rather than positions.

Q: Yet you seem to forget the extreme abuses that dependents have suffered, and continue to suffer, at the hands of natural persons. Incest, visited by fathers upon their daughters, is one example, although there are many others. Modern institutions have fewer such abuses.

A: I gave examples of extreme psychopathologies and physical abuses; for example, the sexual abuse of farm girls by men on the farm. And there have been studies of the fens in the Midlands of Cambridgeshire, England, which show the depravity of socially isolated rural areas. This stands as something we do not want to return to. But those are not the problems that occupy us today. Those that occupy us today are not the problems of intensity of personal relations, but the opposite, created by the extreme penetration of society by corporate actors, problems of neglect and inattention of persons by persons.

Q: Suppose we pursue your line of reasoning. There are observers, such as Ivan Illich and John Holt, who argue against schools. Illich even argues for the deschooling of society. Do you argue, as your position would suggest, that this would be a beneficial change?

A: I believe the book by Ivan Illich, *Deschooling Society* (1971), and the book by John Holt, *How Children Fail* (1964), contain astute observations about the problems created by the school. Another book that examines these matters is Lewis Dexter's *The Tyranny of Schooling: An Inquiry into the Problem of "Stupidity"* (1964). Dexter argues that so-called "stupidity" of normal children is a problem created by the schools, with their narrow focus on a particular kind of learning in a particular kind of relation, the teacher-pupil relation. But the fundamental fallacy behind the notion of deschooling society is the assumption that in the absence of any kind of adult socialization there will not be other influences on children. There will be, and there are, commercial influences from corporate actors intent on satisfying their own interests, as well as the influences of peers no more socialized than the child they are influencing and equally influenced themselves by commercial interests. This solution springs, as do the Moral Majority's solutions, from recognition of certain structural problems that have arisen, but suffers from a similar naiveté about how those problems can be addressed.

Q: Let me change the subject. Perhaps the changes in child rearing that you claim to see are merely the result of a change in the demographic characteristics of our population; that is, the baby boom which created the large cohort of youth beginning in the 1960s.

A: It is true that some of the problems which I have described may have been exacerbated by an abnormally large generation of youth in the 1960s and 1970s. The proportion of persons under age fifteen in western societies has gone down over time, though with some temporary movements up. The generation born in the late 1940s and early 1950s is one such temporary movement. More recently, the downward trend has been resumed. This will dampen some of the phenomena I have discussed but not others. For example, the divorce rate continues up, the number of single-parent households continues up, and I see no signs of reconstruction of the family and its child-rearing capabilities as a result of the decline in numbers of youth relative to adults.

Q: It seems, then, that your projections are linear; that is, you take a linear view of structural changes in society, not one which is more nearly cyclical.

A: You are correct. I do not see cyclical movements that would lead back toward community. You forget the long-term development of modern impersonal corporate actors that I have described. There are certain short-term movements, such as the commune movement in the late 1960s. But the changes in technology and the new form of social structure has brought a liberation that most of us like very much. I see no cyclical movements which will reverse that.

Q: What then will happen, unless we are to become the first species that forgets how to raise its young?

A: As problems generated by the new social structure come to be greater, then we will, in dialogues like this, arrive at ways to achieve a rational modification of the structure. By a rational modification I mean one that combines some of the benefits of the new social structure without some of the costs that it currently imposes upon children.

Q: You have said nothing about the way that changes in the economic structure affect the child rearing capability of society. There has been an increase in service industry, a decrease in manufacturing, and even manufacturing is increasingly being taken over by automation and robots. Will these trends affect the prospects of age-balanced organizations?

A: I believe they will facilitate it. I have tried to get this started at two different places, neither of which was engaged in manufacturing. One was the Rand Corporation, where I was working for the summer. The other was the Russell Sage Foundation when I was there for a year. I tried to get both these organizations to restructure themselves in this way. It is much easier for organizations like those to make such a change than it would be for most manufacturing organizations to do so.

Q: Are there other highly industrialized or postindustrial societies that seem to be coping better with these forces than the United States?

A: As I pointed out, the state paternalism in Europe and the corporate paternalism in Japan are certainly more in evidence than anything comparable in the United States. Whether such corporate paternalism can be carried out in ways that are generally beneficial for children should be examined in some detail. The fact that there are international differences means that there are valuable opportunities for learning through research some answers to the question you raise.

Q: You have given a chilling assessment. Are there not bases for adult responsibility for raising children other than the economic one, and may not those be sufficient to make the family more resilient than you assume it to be?

A: What kind of bases?

Q: For example, the satisfaction of the child-parent relationship.
A: If that were true, then why would it not already have
exhibited itself?

Q: I'm not sure it has not.
A: How?

*Q: There are new ways of parents interacting with children, ways
in which they're collectively trying to solve family problems.*
A: Perhaps. There are forms of social organization which
are really very promising. My two older sons each spent two
summers on a kibbutz in Israel, and I found that both of them
were much more interested in young children after that
period than before. One of them remarked that before that
time he had had very little contact with babies and young
children. He had not for two reasons, one the small size of the
family of which he was a part, and the other the absence of a
close community focused around the neighborhood. Children now have less contact with other children somewhat different in age.

Communal settings, however, do not always provide a
solution. Benjamin Zablocki, one of the foremost students of
communes, has carried out extensive studies of child rearing
in communes. He has studied both traditional religious communes and some of the communes which grew up in the
1960s. He found that the latter set of communes were characterized by inattention to children. The children were no one's
responsibility. These, of course, were communes which were,
in many cases, established by persons rebelling against authority structures. They made a conscious effort not to establish any kind of authority structure. But this absence of authority carries with it the absence of responsibility.

There are many varieties of social forms which we can
develop, and we should be experimenting with these. In
short, we must recognize the consequences for children of the
new social structure and the technological changes that have
helped produce the asymmetric society.

*Q: You suggested an age-balanced corporation as a solution to
some of the problems of child rearing. Yet how can a single organization initiate this?*

A: It can be done by a single organization. I was once approached to direct a government agency that was to be newly established. Normally, I would have had no interest in this, but I toyed with the idea for some time, with the provision that I would do so only if it would be an age-balanced organization. That may have been unrealistic, and an age-balanced Russell Sage Foundation or Rand Corporation might also be unrealistic. But nothing intrinsically makes it so.

Q: But it is quite unrealistic to believe that an organization with budget constraints, especially in the private sector where it is necessary to compete in a market, can assume these welfare responsibilities without some incentive.

A: It is true, I believe, that creating the right incentives, an appropriate reward structure, brings about such organizational innovations. A necessary component of the reward structure for the corporate actor itself—though possibly not sufficient—is as follows: the corporate actor now pays taxes, and the persons who are its agents pay income taxes for transfer payments for certain governmentally supplied social services, such as education and old-age insurance. If an organization directly supplies these services, its taxes, or the taxes of its employees who provide those services should be reduced accordingly.

Q: But what about the reward structure for the individual within such an organization? Why would employees do anything different than they are doing now?

A: Suppose I had been successful at Rand and brought grade school and high school children into Rand running around through the halls. You are asking what would be the incentive for an economist or a mathematician or a secretary at Rand to be involved with those children in any way. Why would they not simply have a segregated school set off in a separate corner of the building with a few persons employed as teachers?

There are two answers to that question. One answer is that there is already a useful device in the modern corporate actor for establishing arbitrary hierarchical reward structures. That is the bureaucratic authority structure. So all that is

necessary, if we are willing to use it, is to establish a requirement that each person, as part of the job for which that person is paid, spend a certain fraction of time in some social
service activity. That is one answer. I think this is not wholly
satisfactory because people find many ways to dodge or distort an activity which is not intrinsically rewarding. The other
answer is to so structure the interpersonal relations so that
they are rewarding. Some requirements are, in the case of
adult care for and teaching of children, that there be small
numbers of children involved with any one adult, and that the
involvement either have high intensity, if it is over a short
period of time, or continue for a long period.

*Q: I am dubious about corporations taking over social services.
When corporations are involved in such things as the arts, they tend to
oppose the content of the art if it's not to their liking or if it is too
political or too controversial. Wouldn't such a tendency induce people
to act very circumspectly in order to get these services, so that things
like lobbying for welfare rights, social security, and the like will not be
allowable?*

A: The *level* at which these services are to be provided
would still be determined by elected officials; that is, by the
state. The *way* they would be provided would be determined
by the individual corporate actor. An essential virtue of such a
pluralistic system is that those who receive such services can
choose the way they want their services delivered. For example, a child and parents could decide which of a range of
possible settings was best. This would put resources in the
hands of the person rather than the state or the corporation.

⟡ 5 ⟡

Information Rights
in Social Decisions

I HAVE EXAMINED, in these chapters, the nature of a singular change which has occurred in modern society: the growth of large corporate actors which exist without a human being as their ultimate referent. These impersonal corporate actors are modern corporations, trade unions, voluntary associations, and last but not least, the state itself. When they are large in size — and it is only the large corporate actors that interest us here—they ordinarily take on the internal form of bureaucracy, though interesting variations on that have begun to emerge in recent years. Their external relations can be loosely classified into two: relations with other corporate actors, and relations with natural persons like you and me. To use the classification of Chapter 1, these are relations of types 3 and 2, respectively. Both are unlike the dominant relations in societies of the past, the relation that we often continue to regard as the only form of social relation, that is, relations between two natural persons.

Relations of type 2, between natural persons and corporate actors, are particularly problematic, because they have a structural asymmetry: they are between two actors of different types. When the corporate actor is very large, then the asymmetry in type of actor is augmented by an asymmetry of size and numbers. This asymmetry of size and numbers has the potential for making imbalanced the effective rights in the relationship, even when the legal rights of the natural person on one side of the relation and the corporate actor on the other are precisely equal. Because of this, the proclivity of the law for extending the rights of natural persons to the "fictional persons" which corporate actors constitute can have the effect of creating an imbalance in the effective rights of these two parties. In brief, it can have the effect of reducing the rights of natural persons in interaction with large corporate actors. And one of the principal ways it can do so is through imbalances in information.

I want to examine the place of information in two kinds of relations that natural persons have with corporate actors. One of these is the market relation, the relation between a corporate actor as seller and a person as buyer. A second is the relation between a corporate actor and those natural persons who are its sovereigns, that is, those persons who according to constitutional intent have ultimate authority over its action. The most common example is the relations between the state as a corporate actor and its citizens, in the control of its actions.

ASYMMETRY OF INFORMATION IN MODERN MARKETS

Throughout the first half of this century, and particularly in the 1920s and 1930s, a major structural change was occurring in the United States. This was a change which shifted the nation from a set of local communities, largely internally focussed, to a nation in which the focus was no longer local but national. Manufacture changed in many product areas from local firms selling to local markets, to national firms selling to national markets. Washing machines, made by a few national firms, replaced washtubs and washboards, made and sold locally. Breakfast cereals, heralded by entrepeneurs with persuasive public relations skills, replaced locally cracked wheat and oats cooked by mothers each morning. National auto manufacturers emerged in the 1920s and 30s, from the plethora of local auto makers which began all over the country.

Perhaps most important, however, was the emergence of national media of communication. The national magazines were an important medium, gaining their growth in the thirties. Radio was a second medium of importance. And movies were a third. These media first of all were the diffusion mechanisms for the new nationally marketed goods. Through their advertising, they created national markets which facilitated national manufacture. And they themselves had national markets, focusing attention of the population as a whole on common objects of attention.

One of the consequences of this change was that a need for a new kind of information arose for producers. The need was related to the national markets and national audiences— in short, a need for information about markets and audiences.

Producers no longer had direct and informal contact with their customers; they were too far removed. The structural distance between producer and consumer had begun to transcend the ability of persons to informally assess their market, assimilate information about it, and plan on the basis of that. Advertising grew, but advertising was a shot in the dark, and advertisers needed some knowledge of their audience.

Mass communications media, especially radio, were in a similar situation. The electronic medium had no way of knowing even the size of its audience. And neither national radio nor national magazines knew the composition of their audiences, their attentiveness, their interests.

These newly emergent information needs on the part of the newly national corporations led to the development of new types of applied social research: market research and audience research. This research was addressed to specific decision problems confronting the corporate actor: should a radio program be continued? What was the potential audience for a given product? What made people buy a certain good? How many people were listening to radio, and how did they differ from those not listening? How many people read a given magazine advertisement? What were the kinds of appeals that sold war bonds?

Through the study of questions like these, applied social research came for the first time to be part of an explicit sequence of purposive action in society. The actors were business corporations, and in the sequence of purposive action, market research and audience research constituted the feed-back information which guided the action. What is striking is the way in which this development in applied social research reflects a totally new structural form of society—for there was nothing analogous to market research or audience research in earlier periods, that is, before the 1930s. The applied social research of earlier periods constitutes attempts to study "so-cial problems." For very early examples in Europe, see LePlay (1855), Mayhew (1851), and Booth (1889–91). In fact, socio-logical or social-psychological research was coming to be a part of the new social structure. It occurred first in the United States, for it was in the United States that this new social structure grew most rapidly, and in the United States that the new corporate actors which constituted its elements were themselves expanding most rapidly. (See Lazarsfeld and Stan-ton, 1944, for examples of this research.) But as the social structural change came about in Europe as well, most rapidly after World War II, the so-called "American sociology" began to characterize much of empirical social research in Europe as well. What is paradoxical is that sociologists themselves re-mainly largely unaware, in their theoretical writings, of the massive social change of which the discipline's own research was a part.

Following in the wake of the growth of market research came other kinds of information to aid corporate actors in their type-2 relations — that is, their relations with natural persons. One, which grew with the extent of credit financing, is credit reference bureaus, which provide information about persons applying for credit. Another, which grew with the growth of advertising, is address lists, bought by corporations from associations with membership lists, from subscription lists of magazines, and from other sources, and used prima-rily for direct-mail advertising. As these markets became more complex, with more kinds of action possible (a greater number of communication channels for advertising, new forms of creative financing), additional types of information became useful to guide the actions of firms in their market relations with natural persons, and mechanisms to obtain this information were developed. In general, these could be described as "data-gathering" organizations: in some cases applied social research organizations, and in some cases organizations wholly within the business community. Some of the former were in universities—indeed, the whole enterprise of market research and audience research began at university-applied social research centers. I myself received my research training at the most important of these, the Bureau of Applied Social Research at Columbia University— where Paul Lazarsfeld, fresh from the old social structure that still characterized Europe, and finding himself in New York, the hub of this new social structure in the United States, responded to it with communications research and market research. He saw then, as most sociologists do today, the development of market and audience research as the early stage of modern systematic social research. But what I am suggesting now is that these developments were an element of an emergent social structure—the feedback element for modern corporate actors in their asymmetric relations with natural persons.

Yet something seems strangely missing in all this: is it the case that *only* corporate actors have information needs in this emergent asymmetric social structure? What about the information needs of natural persons in their relations with the new national corporations operating in national markets? How are those information needs satisfied?

Advertising is a first answer. Though it appears odd to say so, since advertising is an activity carried out by corporations in *their* interests, not by persons in their interests, advertising by a producer is, in its broadest sense, the provision of information to consumers to guide their purchases. It is, of course, not disinterested information, for it is under the control of a particular producer. And this is the central difference between the role of advertising in providing information for the consumer and the role of market research in providing information for the producer: *both* are under the control of the producer, which is, in the cases of interest to us here, a corporate actor.

I had occasion to examine this asymmetry in some detail a few years ago (Coleman, 1969) in what first appears to be an unlikely setting: the college admissions market. In this market, colleges (which some persons, though not everyone, would say are a benign sort of corporate actor) are on one side, and high school seniors on the other. When we look at the information surrounding this relation, it consists of, on the one hand, colleges providing information about themselves, to guide the choices which applicants must make among colleges, and applicants providing information about themselves, to guide the choices that colleges must make among applicants. But this apparent symmetry vanishes when we ask who determines what information each will disclose about itself. The colleges largely control the information they disclose about themselves, for that information is provided in the college catalog, a publication that not even the most ardent college admissions office would claim provides systematic unbiased information that allows direct comparisons of colleges. The catalog is, of course, designed to present the best face of the college or university; a student in residence at a college or university, and looking at its catalog, sometimes finds it hard to recognize the college.

Colleges also determine the information to be provided by the applicant: systematic information on an applicant from high school grades, in a format which allows some comparability between students from different high schools, and most comparable of all, scores on a standardized test, the SAT test (or in some colleges, the ACT test) designed by a corporate body—the College Entrance Board—established as an agent of the colleges and controlled by them. To add insult to injury, it is the applicant who must pay CEB to provide the information demanded by the colleges.

Symmetry in this relation would dictate either that this information-providing body, the College Board, would be under the joint control of applicants and colleges, or that there be a separate information-providing body controlled by applicants, with the power to require colleges to provide systematic and directly comparable information on themselves in areas determined by the applicants. Obviously, that does not exist now. The technical capability to provide such information is fully within our grasp, and there are isolated examples of it having been done on a pilot basis; but there is nothing on the applicant's side to provide information about colleges of interest to applicants comparable to the College Board and its technical arm, ETS. If we ask why there is not, the answer points to a fundamental asymmetry in the market relation between persons and corporate actors, an asymmetry that holds not merely in this case, but in the broad range of such markets throughout the economy. On one side of the relation, the natural person side, there is what economists call the free rider problem, while on the other side, the corporate actor side, that problem is either nonexistant or easily solved. That is, information that persons would obtain, for example about the products in a market, is of interest to all other persons in that market; but each person's interest is so small and incidental that it is not to the person's interest to pay the costs necessary to obtain the information. Each would like to be a free rider; and unless some organization can be imposed which taxes each person to obtain a sufficient resource to obtain the information, there would exist the paradoxical situation: the information will not be obtained, even though each person would be better off by contributing the resources necessary for obtaining it.

This can be seen even in the few cases in which natural-person consumers have been able to organize to provide information not under producers' control. Consumers' Union, which publishes the magazine *Consumer Reports,* is the best example. The organization would very likely not have come into existence were it not for parentage by consumer cooperatives. And it is always subject to the threat that if the cost of the publication is too high, a consumer actively interested in a given product may go to the public library to read the relevant issue rather than subscribing — thus becoming a free rider. It is to the interest of each to do this, despite the fact that if all do there will be no magazine, and all will be worse off. On the other side of the relation, the corporate actors are first of all much more heavily interested in this market, for it may be their major activity; they are fewer in number and thus more capable of organizing, as, for example, the elite colleges in the United States did some eighty years ago to form the College Board as their joint agent, or the electronic media did in spawning the Nielsen ratings, or magazines did in bringing into existence the audited circulation data, or as other industries have done through the multitude of information services that can be found in the libraries of any business school. And in some case, the information desired by the corporation, and obtained by it through market research, is not a public good subject to the free-rider problem at all, but a private good. That is, it is information about consumers' response to its *own* product, or is, in another way, information which is designed for its own particular purposes — such as for the design of an advertising campaign.

In such a circumstance, there will be information generated on one side of the relation, under the control of actors on that side, but little or no information on the other side, under control of the actors on that side.

It is in such a situation that a solution through the state becomes attractive, for the state already taxes persons and thus has solved the free-rider problem. And we find that, in fact, the state is the principal means through which impartial information of interest to consumers is provided — either through its coercive process, as in the imposition of labelling or truth-in-lending or other disclosure requirements upon producers in various markets, or through consumer research or ombudsman activities. A major defect of this solution is that there is no automatic way of knowing whether an action by the state, such as a labelling law, accurately reflects the interests of the natural persons who are citizens of the state. Is it worth the cost to print nutritional information on food packages? Perhaps, but I think no one really knows. Another major defect is that the state has very imperfect ways of discovering just what information would be of value to consumers. As a result, we remain unaware of the potentially valuable forms of information for consumers that remain unavailable because those whose interests would be served are too fragmented to bring into being the corporate actors necessary to make it available.

Thus the problem of appropriate social organizations to counteract the existing—and growing—asymmetry in market relations between persons and corporate actors remains only crudely and partially solved. Social inventions may be devised which will come closer to a satisfactory rebalancing of information in this asymmetric relation, but in no society can it be said that there is currently a satisfactory information balance in market relations.*

INFORMATION RELEVANT TO SOCIAL POLICIES OF THE STATE

Turning to information problems in controlling the actions of corporate actors, the actor of most interest is the state, and the actions of most interest are social policies. These policies, at the level of national government, are relatively recent arrivals on the scene, and it is useful first to ask how it is that they have come about. The answer, curiously enough, is related to the change which spawned market research beginning in the 1930s.

In the 1920s, 30s, and 40s, the nation had undergone a change in the structure of social interaction — from a structure that was almost entirely local and personal to one that had a large component of national marketing. World War II provided a stimulus to this change by inducing even more rapid rural-urban migration and more generally by inducing moves away from the locality and even the region of one's birth.

---

*One proposal, which I have long felt was worth exploring, would be to require that for every dollar spent on market research in a given market, a dollar be made available to consumers for consumer research, and for every dollar spent on advertising, a dollar be made available to consumers for dissemination of information about products, but under the control of consumers. The catch to this, of course, is that implementation would require creation of another corporate actor, which would quickly come to represent interests somewhat different from those of consumers — even if consumers' interests could be said to be a single common interest.

A SHIFT IN THE STRUCTURE OF RESPONSIBILITY

This change in the structure of interaction from personal and local to impersonal and national induced, by the 1960s, another change: a change in the structure of responsibility from private and local to public and national. So long as the principal interactions in society were confined to locality and were primarily between persons, the claims that persons exercised for care, attention, and responsibility when they were in need were largely upon those other persons with whom they were in frequent contact. Adult children took care of aging parents; families exercised responsibility for their mentally defective members, within the household; extended families aided out-of-work brothers, uncles, and nephews in their time of need, and provided a home for unmarried members on a continuing basis.

The change in structure of interaction through the rise in national markets brought with it, quite naturally, a change in the structure of responsibility. If two parties are in regular and continuing interaction, they begin to acquire rights in the relationship and can exercise claims on one another. This proposition is generally true in interpersonal interactions; I am asserting here that it is true in interactions between persons and large corporate actors as well. Those interactions may be mediated by mass communications, as in the interactions between persons and "the nation" considered as a body; or they may be mediated by multiple layers in a bureaucracy, as in the relation between employer and employee. But despite their mediated character, rights are acquired and claims come to have legitimacy, creating a structure of responsibility that did not exist in the absence of the continued — though indirect — interaction.

This changed structure of communication increasingly generated claims upon the state, and an assumption by the state of responsibilities that would never have even arisen before the changed structure of interaction.* Certain of these,

---

*An interesting research question is the question of under what conditions the claims of persons come to be upon the state, and under what conditions they come to be upon the corporate actor with which the person is in continu-

such as Social Security and emergency work programs, arose in the 1930s, early in the shift from local to national interaction. These were certainly stimulated by the extent of common need during the Depression, but the problems were responded to by the state as they had not been by earlier depressions.

A particular instance of this change that is of special importance in the United States is that of the black population. Before the war most blacks were located in the rural South. The only claims they could exercise, in the limited structure of interactions characteristic of the country as a whole at the time and especially characteristic of rural areas, was upon their local black community (e.g., through the church) or the farm owner for whom they worked or cropped.

After the war, and after the move to the urban North had taken place for the majority, most blacks were in a national structure of interaction. They bought goods marketed nationally, they were a part of the mass media audience, and they were — as part of this structure of communication — increasingly subjects of mass media attention as well.

The special importance of the case of blacks was that as they became part of the national structure of interaction, a broader set of national responsibilities arose, because of their objectively depressed conditions, and because of past discriminations in local interactions that were helping to maintain those conditions. In the absence of a national structure of interaction, and the national structure of responsibility that grew out of it, those discriminations would have continued as they had in the past. In the presence of the new structure of responsibility, the special claims of blacks provided an additional impetus to national responsibility in areas where claims were once limited to localities (as in education) or to private relations (as in health care, housing, welfare).

This shift in the structure of claims and responsibility was a steady one which not only led persons to increasingly make claims upon the state, but also made the population receptive

---

ing interaction—for example, the employer. Again, Japanese social organization in modern industry would be useful to study with this problem in mind (see Dore, 1973; Clark, 1979).

to new legislation, executive action, and court decisions which accepted the legitimacy of the claims and assumed new responsibilities on the part of the state. Although this increase in claims and receptivity in the population as a whole was a continuous process, the state actions responsive to these changes came in spurts. One was the 1954 Brown decision of the Supreme Court on school desegregation. A second spurt was the "Great Society" legislation of Lyndon Johnson, beginning in 1964: the Civil Rights Act of 1964, the Elementary and Secondary Education Act of 1965, the Office of Economic Opportunity, the Headstart program, Medicare, and a number of others. A third spurt in a somewhat different area came in the 1970s with safety and environmental regulations, with the state taking responsibility and authority in matters of safety and of air and water quality that had previously been seen to be individual or local responsibilities. Air quality in large cities, water quality in some rivers, and industrial occupational hazards had all been worse in earlier periods in this country, but in the absence of a structure of state responsibility, they were not seen as societal problems.

A NEW PHASE OF SOCIAL RESEARCH

As the structure of responsibility changed, the state began to initiate a broad set of social policies — as distinct from economic policies. These were policies in health, education, welfare, employment, as well as regulatory policies. And with these policies came a new kind of social research: social policy research. This research has come to take a number of forms, some with names that were unknown in 1960: large scale social experimentation, process evaluation, product evaluation, formative evaluation, summative evaluation, program evaluation, planned variations, intervention research, national longitudinal studies.

The reasons that social policy at a national level has generated social policy research are several, but it is sufficient to note only one: as the state assumed public responsibility in matters where responsibility had been local and private, it was ill equipped to discharge this responsibility. This inability stemmed largely from the structural distance between the national government and the activities in which it was exercising responsibility—a distance that mirrored the distance and indirectness of a national structure of interaction that had arisen through national markets and national media of communication.

Research was necessary to learn whether a social program should be continued — even whether it was working in the manner intended. Research was necessary to learn how a program should be modified, or if it should be continued at all. Because the policy was at a national level and its execution was at a local level, the old, direct, informal methods of getting such feedback were no longer feasible. And the new methods for obtaining that feedback can be broadly termed social policy research. But the role of social policy research is far from settled.

TWO MODELS FOR THE LOCUS OF POLICY RESEARCH IN SOCIETY

One conception of the role of policy research in society is given by the idea of rational action or by control theory for self-regulating systems. This is a conception of a system with a central governing element which obtains feedback from actions (or "policies") and modifies those actions on the basis of the feedback information it receives. This conception also fits well with the conception of rational or bureaucratic authority. Decision making by bureaucratic authority requires information concerning the outcomes of policies, and when those outcomes are not directly observable, some sort of policy research is necessary to provide that information. Such a conception of the rational functioning of society has been expressed by several social scientists and social philosophers. L. Haworth (1960) develops such a conception and terms it "the experimenting society," seeing it as a desirable model for the future development of society. Jurgen Habermas (1971) sees it also as a model for the future development of society, but an oppressive and dangerous one. His objection lies in its bypassing of politics and the clash of interests which make up politics.

This model of the locus of policy research in society is one implicitly held by most government officials who think of employing policy research, and by many researchers. In particular, it is the model with which economics has operated throughout its history as a policy science. But its principal characteristic should be recognized: it conceives of information fed back to a single central authority. Its compatibility with bureaucratic theory means also compatibility with a monolithic authority structure. It has no place for a conception of different interests, of democratic political systems in which policy decisions come not from above but from a balance of pressures from conflicting interests.

There are numerous examples of this model being used explicitly or implicitly by government officials. One example is that of the negative income tax experiments carried out at various locations in the United States. The first experiment was carried out in New Jersey and analyzed by economists at the University of Wisconsin. The analysis focused principally on the question of labor supply: would the negative income tax (which provided a guaranteed annual income) reduce the amount which people worked, and thus greatly increase the extent of economic dependency in the U.S.? The result was that there was such an effect, but it was small. Those results supported the government's policy proposals for a negative income tax. These results were openly announced and disseminated by the government agency. Later when the Carter administration was attempting to pass a negative income tax bill, the Department of Health, Education, and Welfare called research analysts to testify before Congress, thus allaying fears of some congressmen that there would be a drastic effect in reducing the willingness of people in the lower echelons of the labor force to work.

Another experiment was carried out in Seattle and Denver, and analyzed at the Stanford Research Institute. Sociologists at SRI found a surprising result: the negative income tax sharply increased divorce rates and reduced remarriage rates. These results, which were more helpful to opponents of the government policy, were treated very differently by HEW. The reports were subjected to extensive challenge, reports were buried rather than disseminated, and HEW did not call the researchers to testify before Congress. The results gained wide attention only after some members of Congress learned of the results and independently called for testimony on the results.

The reasons for the different treatment of these two research results are several. One is institutional: the Institute for Research on Poverty at the University of Wisconsin and the Assistant Secretary for Planning and Evaluation (ASPE) at the Department of HEW had very close ties, with some circulating membership; this was not true for the relation between ASPE and the SRI researchers. Thus there was a high level of trust and similarity of viewpoint at IRP and ASPE. A second reason was disciplinary; ASPE and IRP were staffed largely by economists, and the labor-supply results were obtained by IRP economists using standard econometric methods. The SRI researchers were sociologists and were using mathematical methods of analysis that the IRP and ASPE economists only slowly came to understand and accept.

But I suspect the most important reason had to do with HEW's governmental policy role: it was the designer and promulgator of the administration's negative income tax bill. Thus it was interested principally in those research results which showed the benefits of NIT or allayed fears about its harm. It was not interested in disseminating research results which would help defeat the bill (as, in fact, the divorce results, once disseminated, did). Thus HEW had a strong interest in preventing open dissemination of certain research results. In short, HEW was interested in the use of research results not primarily to influence policy but primarily to help sell a policy already designed. Consequently, it was willing to suppress or ignore those results which were not helpful toward this goal.*

There is, however, another model for social policy research. This second model of the locus of policy research in society, which might be termed the model of "pluralistic policy research," is sharply different. It begins with a conception of interested parties (a conception foreign to the ethic of objectivity that is ordinarily seen to govern research in a scientific discipline), and it conceives of those interests shaping policy research at two points: in formulating research problems to be studied and in receiving the research results. According to this model, objectivity enters in execution of the research but does not govern the posing of the problems or the use of the results. Rather, results are used by interested parties in pursuit of their interests. This model conceives of research results not as providing an objective truth which then is implemented by the policy maker. Rather, it regards policy as the resultant of a balance among conflicting values and interests. The other model, the "policy maker-as-rational-actor" model, implicitly assumes that there are no fundmental conflicts of interest, and then when research has clarified consequences of a policy, conflicts will vanish, or at least that there will be an "objectively correct" policy. The pluralistic model assumes multiple rational actors, each with differing interests, each with legitimate partial control of policy, and each with needs for information in order to pursue its interests rationally.

Despite the fact that a model of pluralistic policy research is not explicitly held by most policy makers or policy researchers, components of it have entered into policy research in various ways. The example of the negative income tax research results on divorce and remarriage illustrates one way,

---

*An investigative and auditing agency of Congress, GAO, investigated the role of ASPE in this case. They concluded that there was no intentional suppression of the report but only "lack of communication" between levels of the agency. But one is led to wonder why there was lack of communication concerning this result but not concerning the results favorable to the policy. One is also led to wonder whether GAO's "adversary role" vis-à-vis executive branch agencies is played as fully as it would be if GAO were not part of the same large corporate actor, the state.

despite the fact that it was unintended by the governmental agency. In that case, the research results, both those that were helpful to the government agency proposing the bill and those that were helpful to its opponents, were presented in a congressional committee, which is one of the principal arenas in the United States government for expression of differing interests. As a different kind of example, the design of research that is mandated by Congress sometimes begins by an attempt to discover the "intent of Congress," an activity which can locate multiple and conflicting intents on the part of different congressmen.* There have increasingly come to be suggestions that "secondary analysis" of policy research be carried out by different researchers, and some secondary analyses have been done with differing policy implications. (For an example involving the effects of Sesame Street, see Ball and Bogatz, 1969; and Cook et al., 1975.) There have been proposals for a "science court" to adjudicate conflicting scientific evidence presented by opposing interests; and there have been suggestions that two or more research projects be carried out on the same topic guided by differing interests (see Task Force of the Presidential Advisory Group, 1976; and Coleman, 1972, respectively). In a number of cases in which research was concerned with strongly contested policy, the original data have been reanalyzed by several researchers with the aim of discovering flaws in the original analysis and possibly differing results. (For example, see Coleman et al., 1966; Cain and Watts, 1970; Hanushek and Kain, 1972; Cicarelli et al., 1969; Campbell, 1971; Page and Keith, 1981; and Coleman, 1981.)

The pluralistic model also accords with the actual use made of some policy research. In a number of cases (research on Headstart, research on school desegregation, research on school effects, criminological research), the results have been used not by an administrator or by a government agency but

---

*At least one policy research project carried out such an activity with the indicated result. This led in turn to interviews with various interested parties to learn how their interests could be addressed in the research (see Coleman, 1972).

by interested parties in the public debate surrounding the policy. In fact, it can be argued that such research has more often been used by outside parties *opposed* to the policies of an administrative authority, to provide a "window" into an activity that would otherwise be hidden by administrative interests. Research often finds that the effectiveness of a policy does not match the claims for it and thus gives legitimacy to opposition to that policy.

The divorce results of the negative income tax experiments are an example of this. In the model of pluralistic policy research, then, the societal effects of the research may be exactly opposite to those envisioned by Haworth and feared by Habermas. Policy research pluralistically formulated and openly published may strengthen the hand of those interests without administrative authority, by redressing the information imbalance between those in authority and those outside. The dangers of this pluralistic policy research, if any, are to *weaken* central authority vis à vis outside interests, not to strengthen it.

It is not clear just how policy research will develop, which of these two models will predominate. What is clear, however, is that the answer to this question affects the future of political pluralism. The matter is, in effect, truly a question of political theory. The political theorists responsible for the American Constitution — Hamilton, Madison, Jefferson, and others — contemplated a smaller society composed primarily of natural persons, with fewer, smaller, and more personalized corporate actors, a society in which relations were far more symmetric than in the social structure we inhabit today. In that society representation of various interests in decision making was of central importance to political pluralism, as of course, such representation is today. And the institutions of government, with representative assemblies such as the Congress, and with a balance of power between different branches of government, were designed to insure fair representation of the various interests. But there were few information problems in that society, a society in which relations had not yet become highly asymmetric. Consequently, the conceptions of *interests and rights with regard to information* were primitive and existed primarily in a passive form: the guarantee of freedom of speech. Beyond that, toward a conception of rights of citizens to certain kinds of information, there was almost nothing. Only recently, principally in the decade of the 1970s, has attention been directed to these matters by legislation, the most important of which is the Freedom of Information Act. Yet this act and the various other "information rights" acts are largely ad hoc and poorly informed by a political theory of information rights—principally because of the near absence of political theory of information rights. Thus if I have one prescription for work in political theory, it is toward the development of a political theory of information rights. As I see it, there would be two major branches in that theory: one concerning information rights in market relations between two independent actors—one large and one small—and the other concerning information rights for the sovereign citizens of a state who have both authority and responsibility for controlling the actions of the state. In this important area political theory is more than an academic exercise; it can, when well developed, provide the prescriptions for a set of political institutions that will restore the balance that in smaller societies existed naturally. Until that time some aid is provided by a more explicit recognition of the structural asymmetry of modern society and its implications for the information which two parties to a relation have. That explicit recognition is what I have tried to bring about in this chapter.

DIALOGUE 5

Q: You examined information rights in market relations and in the relation between citizens and the state, but you were silent on information rights within a bureaucracy—within a modern corporate actor, if you will.

A: That is true. I will try to partially remedy that now. Some time ago I examined this in the context of school systems. What I set out to do was to devise a computerized information system for schools to provide attendance data, grade sheet data, and other information that would help a school administratively, to be done with a few terminals and a small computer in a school. (See Coleman and Karweit, 1972, for the results of this attempt.) In trying to carry out such an activity, I came very quickly to the recognition of a central question: who had rights to what information? Other people had come to that conclusion long before I did, but the question, "who should have rights to particular kinds of information concerning particular students and particular teachers?" was central. For example, who should have rights to information concerning achievement, attendance, and behavior of the students of a particular teacher, information which could be used to make some judgment about the qualities of that teacher? In a traditional authority structure all such rights existed at the top. That kind of wholly centralized authority system no longer exists in most organizations. What becomes problematic is the relation between the structure of information rights and the structure of authority in the system. Just as there exists little in the way of political theory of information rights in a democratic political system, there exists little theory concerning information rights of natural persons who occupy positions in a modern corporate actor. The information rights legislation of the 1970s created some new rights, such as the right to review one's personnel records, for governmental employees. But the area as a whole is in a primitive state.

Q: I would like to return to your example of the negative income tax experiment and the information that the experiment led to an increase in divorce and reduced remarriage. One might say, "Well, that is sufficient evidence for them to abandon the policy," but I believe it is not. It is more information, but more information did not necessarily lead to a better policy.

A: I believe it did in this case, or rather prevented initiation of a bad policy. Most Americans would not favor a policy which led to such a massive destruction of low-income families, as predicted by this research. Let me describe what seems to be going on to produce these divorces. Suppose a woman who has a number of children and is not in the labor market (and therefore does not have an income of her own) has a choice between two spouses. One, her current spouse, is at times warm and sexually rewarding. He sometimes has an income and at other times has no income. He is unreliable, sometimes argumentative, sometimes drunk, and sometimes even beats her. She has an offer from another potential spouse, one who is not sexually rewarding but provides a steady income. This one is highly impersonal but does not beat her, and, in fact, leaves her completely alone. Some women probably would choose the second; some would choose the first. The evidence from interviews with people in the negative income tax experiment suggests that what the guaranteed annual income did for some women whose marriages were not very satisfactory, was to provide an offer from an alternative spouse, whom they had known as Uncle Sam.

Were these women who chose Uncle Sam instead of their present spouse better off, and were their children better off? Possibly, but possibly not. The new policy would have provided (as other evidence indicates current welfare policies have already provided) the state as an alternative to the family, as a means for the distribution of income among dependents. Before such a policy, with extensive consequences for the one communal unit on which every society has depended, is carried out it seems wise to examine its longer-term and indirect consequences. The large increase in single-parent households in recent years seems, in view of the effects of the new social structure on child rearing which I examined in Chapter 4, sufficient indication that a policy like this should not be lightly entered into. What seems warranted here is exploration of other possible policies, including those which might improve the functioning of families rather than destroy the bad ones.

Q: But this research did not provide information about such policies. It merely provided information which helped kill the proposed policy.

A: I have a conception of social policy research that is very similar to the conception of a weapon in a war. A social policy research result, such as the divorce result in the negative income tax experiment, is like the invention of a new weapon. Those who see it as beneficial to their policy stances use it, and those whose policy stance is harmed by it attempt to discredit it. (In the negative income tax experiment, the latter group included free-market economists whose theory led them to favor the policy.) We have a misconception when we think that there is dispassionate use, or even that there *should* be dispassionate use, of social policy research. I think that we should think of social policy research as providing a different starting point. The divorce result may have so strengthened the hand of opponents to the policy that it prevented the bill's passage, but what it does in the longer run is to provide a more enlightened starting point for information about the effects of different forms of transfer payments in modern society. There is a higher level of understanding than existed before the negative income tax experiments.

Q: You described how the movement in markets toward national relations between persons and large corporate actors led to the assumption by government of more and more responsibilities. This meant that the government began to collect more information about individual citizens. This seems to have created an extensive information imbalance.

A: Much of the impetus behind the Freedom of Information Act was exactly directed at correcting that imbalance. The imbalance lies in the fact that a large corporate actor, whether it was the state or a credit bureau or a still different actor, could obtain extensive dossiers on persons. Yet the Freedom of Information Act and other information-related legislation of the 1970s was, as I indicated, uninformed by a political theory of information rights. Before the appropriate restructuring occurs, more work on this aspect of political theory is necessary. I have given only a glimpse of the necessary directions here.

Q: Has there been any investigation of potential conflict between freedom of information and the right to privacy, as, for example, when those two requirements are faced by the people who are attempting to employ others in the Civil Service?

A: There has been some examination of this. A conference at the University of Chicago Law School examined exactly this, and the papers in the conference have recently been published (Posner, 1980). I was impressed during that conference by the fact that the laws which have been introduced in recent years dealing with information have very sharply differentiated between persons and corporate actors. They have been laws which have provided rights to privacy for natural persons but a reduction of privacy rights for corporate actors. One might see these laws as a reaction of natural persons to the information asymmetry. Almost all of these laws can be seen as directed against corporate actors on behalf of natural persons. This, of course, can create conflicts of the sort you described, between the interests of persons in their capacity as agents of a corporate actor (for example, in hiring other persons) and the interests of natural persons (for example, those being hired).

Q: Consider the asymmetry involved in the following situation. A representative of the United States government comes to me and asks about a former student of mine that the government is interested in employing. Whatever I say can be revealed by the Freedom of Information Act. Yet, what is being requested is something that I'm supposed to say in confidence. That is, my right to privacy is now abridged by my former student's freedom of information. What is going on here?

A: When, as in this case, there are three parties, not two, it is less easy to talk about asymmetry. In this case, two parties, you and the former student, are natural persons, and one, the government, is a corporate actor. What this conflict between freedom rights and privacy rights reflects is the point I made at the very end of the chapter: the Freedom of Information Act, and the other similar acts, have not been informed by a sophisticated political theory of information rights. Thus they lead to conflicts of rights like this one.

Q: The antiestablishment movement of the last generation and a half led to, among other things, the freedom of information acts, in an effort to break down the establishment. Now, many persons from that antiestablishment movement have moved into the establishment. Is there any research to show what kind of corporate actors these persons make?

A: No. But there is some understanding of the sources of the antiestablishment orientation. There appear to have been two sources. One was a demographic phenomenon; namely, the huge bulge in the birth rate. The other was the kind of structural changes in society which had come to impinge on people in a way that had not happened before. In other words, this second source of the antiestablishment activities of the 1970s was a reactionary movement to the modern social developments I have described in this book; that is, the change in the structure of interaction, bringing a new form of social structure. This reactionary movement was in some cases misdirected, in other cases better directed. Both the good and bad directions can be seen in the freedom of information acts.

Q: You seem to believe that social policy research is valuable. But the examples you gave suggest that it merely strengthens disagreements and exacerbates conflicts.

A: You have not seen clearly the role of social policy research in these examples. One major consequence of social policy research is to separate out factual disagreements and the value cleavages, and to settle the factual disagreements even though this may take some amount of analysis and reanalysis. This then allows the value cleavages to rise to the surface. This is an important aid to the democratic process, because it leads each of us to evaluate potential or existing policies more accurately in terms of our values. Disagreement remains, but that is inherent in any collectivity.

Q: John Dewey thought that some kind of experimental logic would be a basis for promoting agreement on social and political issues.

A: I think this is an incorrect, romantic notion.

Q: You have addressed the question of who has access to information in the asymmetric society but not how we decide what kind of information is to be generated. The kind of information I need may be considerably different from the kind of information that the state or a corporation needs.

A: If you examine my statements closely, you will have the answer to that question. To repeat: in social policy research the participation of diverse interests is important at *two* stages in the research. One is in formulating the kind of information that is to be obtained, and the second is in analysis of that information once obtained. For example, I have been engaged in research on high schools which I have obliquely referred to. The government agency which funded this research, the National Center for Education Statistics, provided a period of a year for research design. I took as my task *not* to sit down in my armchair with other sociologists or with government officials and decide what information should be gathered from the students, from the schools, from the teachers. Rather, what we did was to devise a research process in which we attempted to discover three things: first, the policy issues in secondary and postsecondary education; second, the interested parties in those policy issues; and third, through interviews with those interested parties, the information needs they had in order to pursue their interests.

Q: But does that assure that all the interested parties have access to you, since you are the central designer of the information to be obtained?

A: No, it does not insure that, and therefore does not solve the problem fully. Nevertheless, one avenue toward partial solution of the problem is the careful investigation of the various interests in the way I described. If that research is good, it will discover the principal interests and their information needs. This is an important aspect of policy research design, yet one which is seldom recognized. In books on methodology, or in methodology courses or courses on research design, this is not ordinarily discussed. Yet it is a central issue.

Q: You argued for a political theory that would show the appropriate institutions for balancing the information rights of persons and corporate actors. Can such theory be developed? What direction would it take relative to the existing Constitution?

A: One place where the common law began to go wrong (though it was not wrong so long as there was no structural asymmetry) was when it began to treat fictional persons and natural persons alike. We must go back to that point to look at the rights, to see how those rights might be differentiated in terms of the other resources that the parties bring to a transaction. This would lead either to a different kind of precedent in common law or a changed structure of statutory law, to differentiate between rights, depending upon the other resources the actor brings to the transaction. Beyond that I will not venture.

Bibliography

Austin, John. *The Province of Jurisprudence Determined,* ed. H. L. A. Hart. London: Weidenfeld and Nicholson, 1954 (1879).

Ball, S., and Bogatz, G. A. *The First Year of Sesame Street: An Evaluation.* Princeton, N.J.: Educational Testing Service, 1969.

Bentley, Arthur. *The Process of Government.* Chicago, Ill.: University of Chicago Press, 1908.

Berle, Adolph A., and Means, Gardiner. *The Modern Corporation and Private Property.* New York: Macmillan, 1940.

Berman, Harold J., and Quigley, John, Jr., trans. and eds. *Basic Laws on the Structure of the Soviet State.* Cambridge, Mass.: Harvard University Press, 1969.

Blau, Peter. *Exchange and Power in Social Life.* New York: Wiley, 1964.

Bloch, Marc. *Feudal Society,* vol. 1. Chicago, Ill.: University of Chicago Press, 1961.

Booth, Charles. *Life and Labour of the People,* 12 vols. 1889–91; London: Macmillan, 1902–1903.

Bradburn, Norman M., and Caplovitz, David. *Reports on Happiness.* Chicago, Ill.: Aldine, 1965.

Bronfenbrenner, Urie. *Character* 2, no. 2 (December 1980).

Brown, Michael. *Laying Waste: The Poisoning of America by Toxic Chemicals.* New York: Pantheon Books, 1980.

Burt, Ronald S. "Corporate Society: A Time Series Analysis of Network Structure," mimeographed. Chicago, Ill.: National Opinion Research Center, 1975.

CAA Cancer Journal for Clinicians 30, no. 1 (January–February 1980).

Cain, Glen, and Watts, Harold. "Problems in Making Policy Inferences from the Coleman Report." *American Sociological Review* 35 (1970): 228–42.

Campbell, Donald. "Methods for the Experimenting Society." Paper presented at the meeting of the American Psychological Association, Washington, D.C., September 1971.

Chandler, Alfred D., Jr. *The Visible Hand: The Managerial Revolution in American Business.* Cambridge, Mass.: Harvard University Press, 1977.

Cicarelli, Victor, et al. *The Impact of Head Start.* Springfield, Va.: U.S. Clearinghouse for Federal Scientific and Technical Information, 1969.

Clark, Rodney. *The Japanese Company.* New Haven, Conn.: Yale University Press, 1979.

Coleman, James S. "Female Status and Premarital Sexual Codes." *American Journal of Sociology* 72, no. 2 (September 1966): 217.

———. "The Symmetry Principle in College Choice." *College Board Review,* no. 73 (Fall 1969), pp. 5–10.

———. *Methods of Policy Research.* Morristown, N.J.: General Learning Press, 1972.

———. "Response to Page and Keith." *Educational Researcher* 10, no. 7 (August/September 1981): 18–20.

———, et al. *Equality of Educational Opportunity.* Washington, D.C.: U.S. Government Printing Office, 1966.

———, and Karweit, Nancy L. *Information Systems and Performance Measures in Schools.* Englewood Cliffs, N.J.: Educational Technology Publications, 1972.

Commons, John R. *The Legal Foundations of Capitalism.* New York: Macmillan, 1924.

Cook, Thomas D., et al. *"Sesame Street" Revisited.* New York: Russell Sage Foundation, 1975.

Denman, D. R. *Origins of Ownership.* London: Allen & Unwin, 1958.

Dexter, Lewis. *The Tyranny of Schooling: An Inquiry into the Problem of "Stupidity."* New York: Basic Books, 1964.

Dore, Ronald P. *British Factory–Japanese Factory: The Origins of National Diversity in Industrial Relations.* Berkeley, Calif.: University of California Press, 1973.

Fremont-Smith, Eliot. "Love Canal — Just a Tragic Occident." *The Village Voice*, June 2, 1980, p. 35.

Fuller, Lon L. *The Morality of Law*, rev. ed. New Haven, Conn.: Yale University Press, 1969.

Gierke, Otto von. *Political Theories of the Middle Ages*, F. W. Maitland, trans. Cambridge: Cambridge University Press, 1968 (1900).
————. *Natural Law and the Theory of Societies*. Cambridge: Cambridge University Press, 1934.

Grossman, Naava Binder. "A Study of the Relative Participation of Persons and Corporate Actors in Court Cases," mimeographed. Chicago, Ill.: National Opinion Research Center, 1974.

Habermas, Jurgen. *Toward a Rational Society*. London: Heinemann, 1971, pp. 106–107.

Hacker, Andrew. *The Corporation Take-Over*. New York: Harper & Row, 1964.

Hanushek, Eric, and Kain, John F., "On the Value of *Equality of Educational Opportunity* as a Guide to Public Policy." In F. Mosteller and D. P. Moynihan, eds., *On Equality of Educational Opportunity*. New York: Random House, 1972, pp. 116–45.

Hart, H. L. A. *The Concept of Law*. Oxford: Oxford University Press, 1961.

Haworth, L. "The Experimenting Society: Dewey and Jordan." *Ethics* 71 (1960): 27–40.

Hayek, Friedrich A. *Law, Legislation, and Liberty*, vol. 1. London: Routledge and Kegan Paul, 1973.

Hirshman, A. O. *Exit, Voice, and Loyalty*. Cambridge, Mass.: Harvard University Press, 1971.

Holt, John. *How Children Fail*. New York: Pitman, 1964.

Illich, Ivan. *Deschooling Society*. New York: Harper & Row, 1971.

Kneese, Allen V., and Schultze, Charles L. *Pollution, Prices, and Public Policy*. Washington, D.C.: Brookings Institution, 1975.

Laski, Harold. *Studies in the Problem of Sovereignty*. New Haven, Conn.: Yale University Press, 1917.

Lazarsfeld, Paul F., and Stanton, Frank. *Radio Research 1942–43*. New York: Duell, Sloan, and Pearce, 1944.

LePlay, Frederick. *Les Ouvriers Européens,* 6 vols., 2d ed. 1855; Tours-Mame: 1855–79.

Levine, Edward M. "The Declining Educational Achievement of Middle Class Students, the Deterioration of Educational and Social Standards, and Parents' Negligence." *Sociological Spectrum* (1980): pp. 17–34.

Lipset, S. M., Trow, M. A., and Coleman, James S. *Union Democracy.* New York: Free Press, 1956.

McPherson, C. B. *The Political Theory of Possessive Individualism: Hobbes to Locke.* London: Oxford University Press, 1962.

Maitland, Frederic. *Trust and Corporation.* Vienna: Alfred Holder, 1904.

Malamud, Bernard. *The Assistant.* New York: Farrar, Straus, and Cudahy, 1957.

Mayer, P. J. *Max Weber and German Politics.* London: Faber and Faber, 1943.

Mayhew, Henry. *London Labour and the London Poor.* 1851; London: Griffin, 1861.

Merton, Robert K. "The Bureaucratic Personality." In R. K. Merton et al., eds., *Reader in Bureaucracy.* New York: Free Press, 1952.

Michels, Robert, *Political Parties.* New York: Free Press, 1949.

Milgram, Stanley. *Obedience to Authority: An Experimental View.* New York: Harper & Row, 1974.

National Safety Council. *Accident Facts,* 1979.

Noll, Roger. "Breaking Out of the Regulatory Dilemma: Alternatives to the Sterile Choice." *Indiana Law Journal* 51, no. 3 (1976): 686–99.

Page, Ellis B., and Keith, Timothy Z. "Effects of U.S. Private Schools: A Technical Analysis of Two Recent Claims." *Educational Researcher* 10, no. 7 (August/September 1981): 7–17.

Pollock F., and Maitland, Frederic W. *The History of English Law,* vol. 1, 2d ed. Cambridge: Cambridge University Press, 1898.

Posner, Richard, ed. Special issue on privacy in economics and law, *Journal of Legal Studies* 9 (December 1980).

Schon, Donald A. *Beyond the Stable State.* London: Maurice Temple Smith, 1971.

Stone, Christopher D. *Where the Law Ends: The Social Control of Corporate Behavior.* New York: Harper & Row, 1975.

Task Force of the Presidential Advisory Group on Anticipated Advances in Science and Technology. "The Science Court Experiment: An Interim Report." *Science* 193 (August 20, 1976): 653–56.

Teitenberg, Thomas H. "Transferable Discharge Permits and the Control of Stationary Source Air Pollution: A Survey and Synthesis." *Land Economics* 56 (1980): 391–416.

Thompson, Dennis F. "Moral Responsibility of Public Officials: The Problem of Many Hands." *American Political Science Review* 74 (1980): 905–918.

Ullman, Walter. *The Individual and Society in the Middle Ages.* Baltimore, Md.: Johns Hopkins University Press, 1966.

U.S. Bureau of the Census. *Historical Statistics of the United States, Colonial Times to 1970.* Washington, D.C.: U.S. Bureau of the Census, 1976.

U.S. Public Health Service. *Health United States.* Hyattsville, Md.: Department of Health, Education, and Welfare, Public Health Service, Office of Health Research Statistics and Technology, National Center for Health Statistics, 1979.

———. *Monthly Vital Statistics Report* 28, no. 13 (November 13, 1980).

Washington Post, February 27, 1980, p. A18.

Weitzman, Lenore. "Legal Regulation of Marriage: Tradition and Change." *California Law Review* 62 (July–September 1974): 1169–288.

Williamson, Oliver. *Markets and Hierarchies.* New York: Free Press, 1975.

Wu, Shi Chang. "Distribution of Economic Resources in the United States," mimeographed. Chicago, Ill.: National Opinion Research Center, 1974.

Wynne, D. *Character* 1, no. 1 (1979).

Young, Michael, and Willmott, Peter. *Family and Kinship in East London.* New York: Free Press, 1957.

Zablocki, Benjamin. *Alienation and Charisma: A Study of Contemporary American Communes.* New York: Free Press, 1980.

Index

The Asymmetric Society

was composed in 10-point VIP Baskerville and leaded two points
by Utica Typesetting Company, Inc.,
with display type in Foundry Baskerville by J. M. Bundscho, Inc.;
printed by sheet-fed offset on 55-pound, acid free Glatfelter Antique Cream,
Smythe-sewn and bound over boards in Joanna Arrestox B,
also adhesive-bound with Carolina covers printed and laminated
by Philips Offset Co., Inc.,
by Maple-Vail Book Manufacturing Group, Inc.;
and published by

SYRACUSE UNIVERSITY PRESS
SYRACUSE, NEW YORK 13210